TRADITIONAL QUILTS
with **Painless Borders**

Barbara J Eikmeier

That Patchwork Place®

Sally Schneider
Barbara J. Eikmeier

Dedication

To our children: David and Laura, Drew, and Ted Schneider; and Eric and Sarah Eikmeier. Blessed are the children for they shall inherit the quilts!

Acknowledgments

All these people helped us in one way or another to put this book together:

Alice Maffey for friendship, support, and encouragement, and for being on call to help with "unsewing";

Karen Hayes for last-minute help with "Mosaic";

Linda Ballard and Sharyn Craig for sharing Sharyn's method for making bias squares;

Virginia Lauth and Maureen McGee for their fine quilting;

Judy Sogn, Sue Linker, Nancy Koorenny, Cheri Potts, and Sally Broeker, who made the Basket blocks for the Friendship Baskets quilt;

Janet Inglis, whose serendipitous paper shuffling resulted in the Double Twisted Ribbon border;

The Editorial Department at That Patchwork Place for being such wonderful people to work with;

Barbara Weiland, for her friendship and support through these past few years;

Mary Ellen Hopkins, for providing the initial inspiration for a Painless Border;

Carol Sather and P&B Fabrics for providing fabric from their Root of All Madder line for the "Weather Vane" quilt on page 24;

Eric and Sarah, for having faith that this book would someday be finished and your mom would come out of the sewing room;

Dale Eikmeier, you are the wind beneath my wings.

MISSION STATEMENT

We are dedicated to providing quality products and service by working together to inspire creativity and to enrich the lives we touch.

Credits

Editor-in-Chief . . . . Kerry I. Smith

Technical Editor . . . . Janet White

Managing Editor . . . . Judy Petry

Design Director . . . . Cheryl Stevenson

Cover Designer . . . . Cheryl Stevenson

Text Designer . . . . Kay Green

Copy Editor . . . . Liz McGehee

Proofreader . . . . Leslie Phillips

Illustrator . . . . Laurel Strand

Photographer . . . . Brent Kane

Library of Congress Catologing-In-Publication Data
Schneider, Sally.
    Traditional quilts with painless borders / Sally Schneider and Barbara J. Eikmeier.
        p.   cm.
        ISBN 1-56477-203-9
        1. Patchwork—Patterns.   2. Borders, Ornamental (Decorative arts)   3. Patchwork quilts.   I. Eikmeier, Barbara J. II. Title.
    TT835.S3483   1997
    746.46'041—dc21   97-27638
                                                                CIP

Traditional Quilts with Painless Borders
© 1997 by Sally Schneider and Barbara J. Eikmeier

That Patchwork Place, Inc.
PO Box 118
Bothell, WA 98041-0118 USA

Printed in the United States of America
02 01 00 99 98 97   6 5 4 3 2 1

TABLE OF CONTENTS

PREFACE

In my first Painless Borders book, published in 1992, I described an innovative way to construct quilts with complex pieced borders that weren't borders at all; they were blocks that, when sewn into the quilt, looked like pieced borders. Since then, so many new borders kept floating around in my head, I just had to make and share them. I asked my longtime quilting buddy, Barbara Eikmeier, to help me, so, at last, we can share more wonderful Painless Border quilts with quilters all over the world.

Most of these border designs are ones that I saw at quilt shows or in magazines. They were all made the "usual" way: as pieced borders added to the quilt after the center was completed. With some experimentation, I was able to adapt the designs to make them as Painless Borders.

I encourage you to play with the patterns. Try using a different block for the center of the quilt. As long as it is the same size, you can usually make it work. Play with the border elements and design your own Painless Border. But above all, make some of the quilts. You'll love the response of your quilting friends when they see the wonderful borders you have included on your quilts.

Sally

Years ago, Sally called me, out of breath, with a concept for a new book. That concept became *Painless Borders*. As she shared the development of that book with me, my enthusiasm grew until I felt I was as much a part of it as Sally was.

I was impressed with the simple techniques and experimented with the design options. It was exciting to win an award in my local quilt guild's challenge contest in the Original Design category, especially since my quilt was wearing a Painless Border. I am still thrilled each time I make a quilt with a Painless Border. The construction is so easy, yet it looks so complicated.

Sally and I have been friends for many years, and since I had an intimate knowledge of the original Painless Borders, it seemed natural to work together on this project. Throughout the development of this book, we have shared ideas for designs, fabrics, and better ways to construct individual units. We hope that you, the quilter, won't be able to tell where Sally ends and Barbara begins, and vice versa. The saying that "two heads are better than one" holds true; this collaboration brings you the best from both of us.

Barbara

INTRODUCTION

Why are these borders called painless? Pieced borders are beautiful additions to a quilt; they can raise the caliber of a quilt from ordinary to spectacular. But, between the calculator and the sewing machine, something often goes awry. Calculations and cutting might be correct, but pieced borders seldom fit as planned. They are a pain!

The elements of many complex pieced borders are pieced diagonally and added as strips around a central design. By incorporating the elements of the border designs into blocks, and setting all the blocks of the quilt diagonally, you create a quilt with complex pieced borders, but without making complex calculations and sewing unwieldy pieced strips. It's painless!

We did use some guidelines to make the quilts in this book easy to sew. All the pieces used in the border blocks had to be squares, rectangles, or triangles, and all blocks had to be quick-pieced. We chose only pieced block designs for the centers of the quilts, but you can use appliqué blocks too, as long as they are the same size as the border blocks.

Examine the quilt plans. See how easily the blocks go together. Try one. Once you do, you'll never make a quilt without a Painless Border again!

BASIC TECHNIQUES

CHOOSING FABRICS

All the quilt plans in this book have blocks set diagonally with large side setting triangles and corner setting triangles around the outside edges, so there are a few things to consider when choosing fabrics for Painless Borders.

Fabrics with stripes or widely scattered, large motifs don't work well as the outermost fabric in these quilts. In most instances, these borders require that the outer fabric be cut up and reassembled, destroying the continuity of a large print design or causing stripes to run both diagonally and straight. Both of these effects are distracting and displeasing to the eye. Avoid solid colors too, because they make the seams in the outer border more apparent. Stripes and fabrics with large motifs work well in the center blocks. You can even fussy-cut pieces so a motif is centered in a unit.

Small to medium-sized, dense prints work best for outer borders. They hide seams well, so you can hardly tell that the outer borders have many pieces unless you look closely. Heavy quilting also hides seams. Barbara's intricate machine quilting hides the seams on all our quilts.

Use the same criteria when choosing the background fabric for the centers of these quilts. There are seams where people don't expect to see them. To hide them, use a small, dense print or a textured solid for the background.

MAKING STRIP SETS

You can quickly assemble blocks (or parts of blocks) made with squares and rectangles by cutting strips of fabric, sewing them together in a specific order to make a strip set, then cutting the set into pieced units and combining them with other units made the same way. See "All Night Long" on page 25 for a good example of this technique.

1. Sew strips together in the order required for your design. Press the seams toward the darker fabric. Use steam, but press carefully to avoid stretching. Press from the right side first, then turn the set over and press from the wrong side to make sure the seam allowances face in the proper direction all along the strip set.

2. Align a horizontal line of the ruler with a seam, then trim the edge of the strip set. Cut units from the set, using the width specified in the quilt plan.

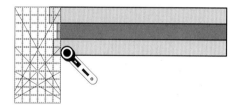

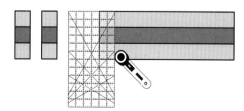

3. Join the units to make the blocks required for your quilt.

◀ *Fabrics in top row are unsuitable for Painless Border quilts. Choose fabrics like those in the bottom row.*

Making Folded Corners

Using the following method, you only need squares to add a triangle to the tip of a square or a rectangle, or to make flying-geese units. Measuring and sewing are simple. You don't even need to draw a sewing line. Although you waste a little fabric, the time and energy saved are well worth it.

1. Place a piece of masking tape on your machine, with the right edge extending in a straight line from the needle toward you. Extend the tape as far toward you as possible. If your machine is portable and doesn't have a wide bed, attach the end of the tape to the table your machine sits on. Trim the tape away from the feed dogs.

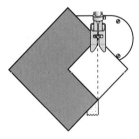

2. Place a small square on one corner of a large square, right sides together, with raw edges even. Begin sewing exactly in the corner of the small square. As you stitch, keep the opposite corner directly on the edge of the masking tape.

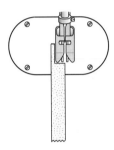

3. Trim ¼" from the seam, then press the triangle toward the corner.

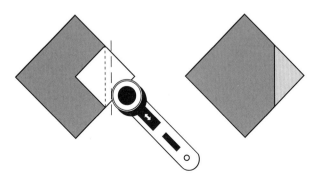

Making Bias Squares

There are probably as many ways to make bias squares as there are teachers. This easy, accurate method was developed by Sharyn Craig.

1. Cut a strip of each of the desired fabrics from selvage to selvage. The width of these strips may vary, depending on the size of the bias square and how much fabric you have. The directions for each quilt tell you the most efficient width to cut the strip.

2. Open the strips to their full width. Place them on the cutting surface as described in the directions for the quilt you want to make. Some strips must be cut right side up, some right side down. Pair bias-square fabric strips right sides together for the most efficient cutting and sewing. Stack pairs of strips if required. Align the 45° mark on the ruler with the bottom edge of the fabric. The side edge of the ruler should intersect the upper left corner of the strip. Cut along the edge of the ruler. Save the corner triangles to make bias squares for scrap quilts.

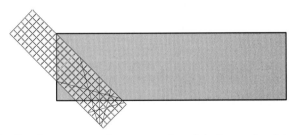

3. Cut bias strips the required width from the fabrics. Refer to the quilt plan or the chart on page 7 to determine the correct size.

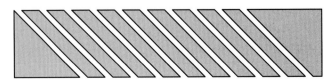

4. Place 2 bias strips, one cut right side up and one cut right side down (or pull pairs of strips from your stacks), right sides together. Stitch along both long edges. Use a generous ¼"-wide seam. Press the stitched strips flat to set the seams.

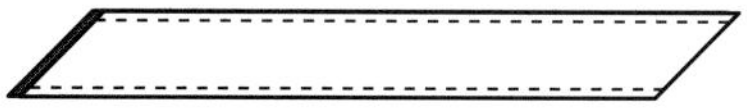

5. Place a bias-strip unit on the cutting surface with the long point on the left side. Line up the diagonal line of a Bias Square® ruler with the left stitching line and trim the excess fabric on the bottom.

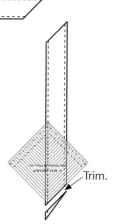

Trim.

6. Move the Bias Square so the diagonal line is on the seam, and the desired cut size (from the chart) is on the trimmed edge. Cut along the edge of the Bias Square ruler.

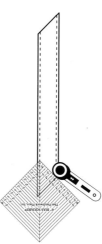

7. Turn the bias strip over and repeat step 6. Continue to flip and cut until you have reached the end of the bias-strip unit. Press the seams toward the darker side and trim the "ears."

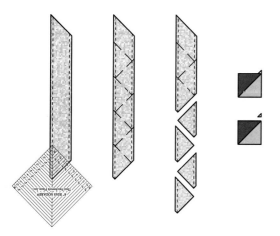

It is not usually necessary to trim the bias strip each time, but if you have made a miscut, you may need to trim again. If your seam allowance was not large enough, you may find a small square cut out of the corner of each bias square. If that happens, resew the bias strip with a wider seam allowance. It is not necessary to rip out the old seam allowance.

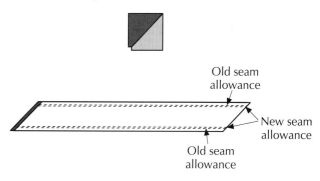

Old seam allowance

New seam allowance

Old seam allowance

Occasionally, if your seam allowance is too wide, you may need to unpick a few stitches from the tip of the triangle. They usually come out easily when you open the bias square.

The chart below will come in handy when you begin designing Painless Borders of your own, or any other time you want to make bias squares.

Finished Size of Bias Square	Cut Width of Bias Strip	Cut Size of Bias Square
1½"	1⅞"	2"
2"	2¼"	2½"
2½"	2⅝"	3"
3"	3"	3½"
3½"	3⅜"	4"
4"	3¾"	4½"
4½"	4"	5"
5"	4⅜"	5½"

Making Quarter-Square Triangle Units

Quarter-square triangle units start with bias squares. Use the chart below to determine the correct size to cut the bias strips.

1. Cut bias strips as required for the size quarter-square triangle unit you need. Construct bias squares, following the directions on pages 6–7.

Finished Size of Quarter-Square Triangle	Cut Width of Bias Strip	Cut Size of Bias Square	Cut Size of Quarter-Square Triangle
2"	2¼"	2⅞"	2½"
2½"	2⅞"	3⅜"	3"
3"	3¼"	3⅞"	3½"
4"	3⅞"	4⅞"	4½"

2. Place 2 bias squares right sides together, alternating the colors. Draw a line diagonally across the bias square, crossing the seam allowance. Stitch ¼" from the line on both sides. Cut on the line.

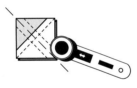

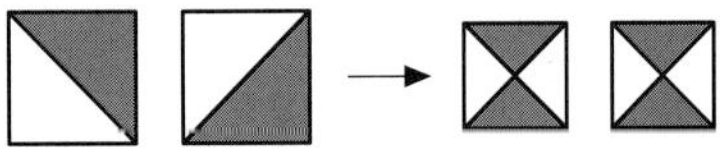

Use two colors to make these squares.

Use three colors to make these squares.

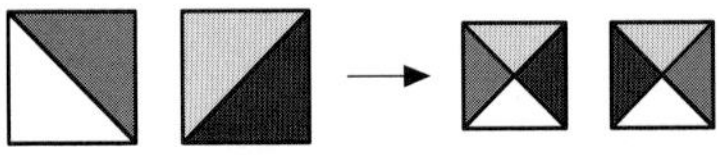

Use four colors to make these squares.

3. To make quarter-square triangle units with 1 large triangle and 2 small ones, cut a square of the fabric for the large triangle the same size as the cut bias square. Place the plain square right sides together with the bias square; draw a diagonal line across the bias square, crossing the seam allowance. Stitch ¼" from the line on both sides, then cut on the line. These units are often required to make a triangle border turn the corner.

Making Mary's Triangle Units

Sally developed this little trick years ago to make Shaded Four Patch blocks quickly.

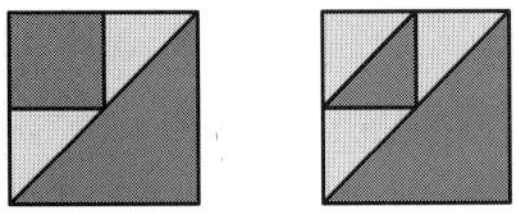

Mary's Triangle Units with squares and with triangles

1. Make bias squares (or cut plain squares) the required size. (See the directions for the quilt you are making.)
2. Cut rectangles 1" longer than the squares. If the squares are 2" x 2", cut the rectangles 2" x 3".
3. Sew a rectangle to a bias square (or square) as shown.

4. Sew pairs of pieced units together. In the center of each unit, clip the seam allowance to the seam line so you can press the seams toward the rectangles as shown.

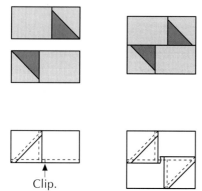

Clip.

5. Cut a square of template material equal to the short edge of the rectangle from step 4. If the rectangle is 4½" x 5½", cut the square 4½" x 4½". Cut the square in half diagonally.

6. Place the template on the wrong side of each pieced rectangle, with the corner of the template on the bias square (or square). Draw a diagonal line across the rectangle unit. Repeat on the opposite corner.

Template   Drawn lines

Template

7. Place each pieced unit right sides together with a same-sized rectangle of another fabric. Sew on both lines, then cut between them. Trim the seam allowance to ¼" if desired. Press the seams toward the larger triangle in each unit.

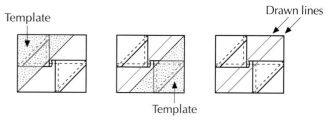

$\mathscr{D}$IAGONAL SETS

All the quilts in this book are set on the diagonal. They are no more difficult to construct than quilts set straight, but there are some important differences. When quilt blocks are set diagonally, there are triangular-shaped spaces around the edges. You must cut side setting triangles and corner setting triangles to fit into those spaces. Always cut them so that the outside edges of the triangles are on the straight of grain to prevent the outer edges of the quilt from stretching. In Painless Border quilts, the outer triangles are often made of several pieces, but the straight of grain should always run along the outer edge.

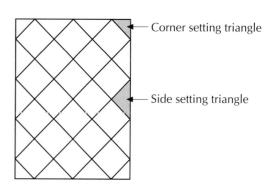
Corner setting triangle

Side setting triangle

MAKING SIDE SETTING TRIANGLES

1. For plain triangles around the edges, measure the diagonal of your finished block.
2. Add 2" to that measurement. Use the new measurement to cut squares of the chosen fabric.
3. Cut the squares twice diagonally for 4 triangles.

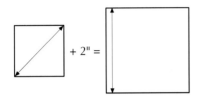 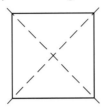

These calculations will yield triangles slightly larger than necessary for your quilt, but for a good reason. When you sew bias edges, the opposite straight edge tends to curve inward. Triangles cut exactly the right size will shrink inward and might end up being too small. It is easy to trim off any extra fabric, but impossible to add more.

Place the side setting triangles in the spaces at the edges of your quilt and sew them to the ends of the rows of blocks, following the diagram below.

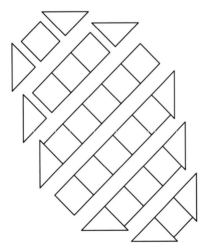

MAKING CORNER SETTING TRIANGLES

For the corner triangles, which you add after sewing the quilt top together, cut two squares, each the same size as the finished blocks in the quilt. Cut the squares once diagonally for four triangles, one for each corner.

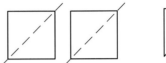

MAKING PIECED EDGE TRIANGLES

Some quilts require pieced edge triangles to allow the border design to flow around the quilt properly. These triangles must also be constructed with the outside edge on the straight of grain.

If a design requires a small triangle on the tip of the side setting triangle, use the folded-corner technique on page 6. Cut a square the required size and place it right sides together on the top corner of the side setting triangle. Align the raw edges and sew diagonally across the square. Trim the square ¼" from the seam and press the triangle toward the corner.

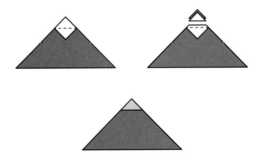

For a design requiring side setting triangles with a complete square at the tip, measure the diagonal of your finished block. Add 2" for the diagonal cuts *plus* another 1" for piecing the square at the tip. If the diagonal measurement of the block is 14", cut the square 17".

Cut a strip from one side of the triangle the same width as the pieced square, *including seam allowances.* Sew the pieced square to the top of the strip, then sew the strip to the triangle and trim off the excess fabric at the bottom. Be sure to cut the strip from the same side of each edge triangle, unless the pattern directs otherwise.

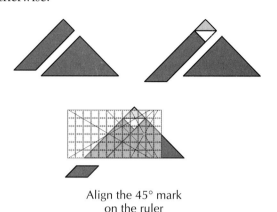

Align the 45° mark
on the ruler
with the seam line.

You can cut more than one strip from the side of a triangle if necessary, but for each cut you make, you must add another 1" to the size of the large square.

ASSEMBLING THE QUILT TOP

To assemble a diagonally set quilt, refer to the quilt plan and the color photo of the quilt you are making. Arrange the blocks, then add the side and corner setting triangles around the edges.

Stand back from the quilt and make sure all the blocks face in the proper direction; it is very easy to turn some of the border blocks the wrong way.

Sew the blocks together in diagonal rows, adding the side setting triangles to the ends of each row. Align the apex of the triangle with the corner of the block.

Trim the corners of the side setting triangles before sewing the rows together.

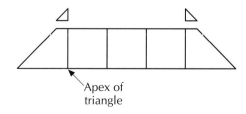

Apex of
triangle

Tip

When you sew bias edges to straight edges, always sew with the bias edge on the bottom to prevent it from stretching.

Sew with the bias edge
on the bottom.

Sew the rows together. We usually construct the quilt in two halves, then join the halves.

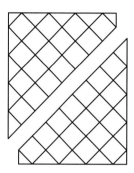

Note
Until a diagonally set quilt is layered and basted for quilting, it is extremely important to use care when handling it. The bias grain of the fabrics runs along the length and width of these quilts. **While layering, be sure to pat the quilt flat rather than push the fullness to one edge.** *Also, take care you do not stretch or distort the fold lines when you fold up the unquilted and unbasted top. You may stretch the center of the quilt so much that it will never lie flat.*

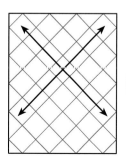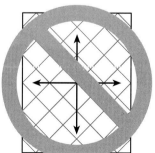

Smooth the quilt top along
the straight grain, not the bias.

Friendship Baskets

Finished Quilt Size: 70" x 70"
Finished Block Size: 10"

White

Assorted prints

Burgundy print

Pink print

Dark green print

Light green print

Materials: 42"-wide fabric

4¾ yds. white print for background

13" x 20" piece each of 13 assorted prints for baskets

Assorted scraps for filling baskets

½ yd. burgundy print for ribbon border

½ yd. pink print for ribbon border

⅜ yd. dark green print for ribbon border

½ yd. light green print for ribbon border

4¼ yds. for backing

75" x 75" piece of batting

⅝ yd. for binding

Cutting

Fabric	No. of Strips	Strip Width	No. of Pieces	Piece Size
Background	2	13"	13 right side up	2⅝"-wide bias strips
	1	5⅞"	13	5⅞" x 5⅞"
	12	3"	32 from 5 strips	3" x 5½"
			33 from 3 strips	3" x 3"
	2	5½"	12	5½" x 5½"
	4	10½"	14	10½" x 10½"*
	2	19"	4	19" x 19" ⊠
Each basket print	1	13"	1 wrong side up	2⅝"-wide bias strips
			1	5⅞" x 5⅞"
Burgundy	4	3"	2 from ½ strip	3" x 8"
			16 from 1½ strips	3" x 3"
Pink	5	3"	16	3" x 10½"
			2	3" x 5½"
			2	3" x 3"
Dark green	3	3"	2 from 1 strip	3" x 8"
Light green	5	3"	2	3" x 8"
			28	3" x 5½"
			12	3" x 3"

*Cut 2 of these squares once diagonally.

⊠: Cut each square twice diagonally.

Block Assembly

1. Referring to "Making Bias Squares" on page 6, pair 2⅝"-wide bias strips of background and basket prints, right sides together. Sew along both long edges. Cut 3" bias squares from the strips. Press the seams toward the darker fabric. You will need 7 bias squares with the same combination of fabrics for each basket.

Make 7 for each basket.

2. Cut each 5⅞" background and basket fabric square in half diagonally. Sew a triangle of each basket fabric to a background triangle as shown. Add the extra triangle of each basket fabric to your scrap basket.

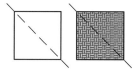

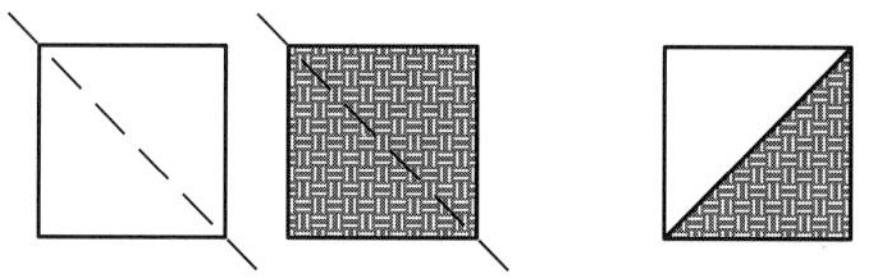

3. Arrange the bias squares and large half-square triangle unit of each basket fabric with a 3" square and 2 rectangles, each 3" x 5½", of background as shown. Sew them together to make a Basket block (Block 1).

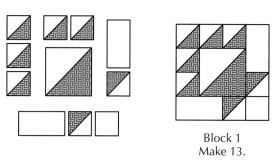

Block 1
Make 13.

4. Appliqué flowers, fruit, or whatever you choose to fill each basket.

1. Using 3"-wide strips of burgundy, dark green, and background, make strip sets as shown.

Make 2.

Make 2.

2. From the burgundy strip sets, crosscut 24 pieces, each 3" wide, and 2 pieces, each 5½" wide. From the dark green strip sets, crosscut 28 pieces, each 3" wide. You may need to make a third short strip set of each combination.

Cut 24.　　　Cut 2.　　　Cut 28.

3. Referring to "Making Folded Corners" on page 6, sew a 3" background square on one end of each 3" x 10½" pink rectangle. Sew background squares on the opposite corners of 2 pink rectangles. Be careful to sew the squares in the direction shown.

Make 8.　　Make 6.　　Make 2.

4. Using the folded-corner technique, sew a 3" background square on one end of a 3" x 5½" pink rectangle in the direction shown.

Make 2.

5. Using the folded-corner technique, sew a 3" light green square on one corner of a 5½" background square.

Make 12.

6. Repeat step 5 with a 3" burgundy square and a 10½" background square.

Block 2
Make 8.

7. Using the folded-corner technique, sew a 3" burgundy square on 2 adjacent corners of a 10½" background square as shown.

Block 3
Make 4.

8. Arrange the folded-corner units with the remaining squares and rectangles to make the border and corner blocks as shown.

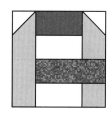
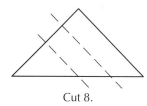

Block 4
Make 2.

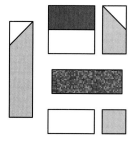
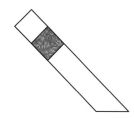

Block 5
Make 2.

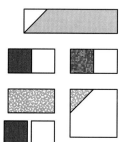
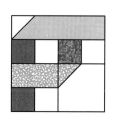

Block 6
Make 6.

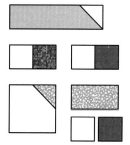
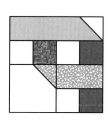

Block 7
Make 6.

1. Cut 2 strips, each 3" wide, from each side setting triangle as shown. Cut 8 in one direction and 8 in the opposite direction.

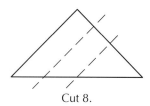

Cut 8.   Cut 8.

2. To the top of the longest strip, add a strip unit from step 2 on page 14.

3. Place a 3" x 5½" light green rectangle at right angles to the square end of the remaining strip as shown. Sew diagonally across the corner. Be sure the pieces face in the direction shown.

Make 8.

Make 8.

Friendship Baskets ◈ 15

4. Reassemble the triangle as shown. Trim the bottom edge even with the small triangle.

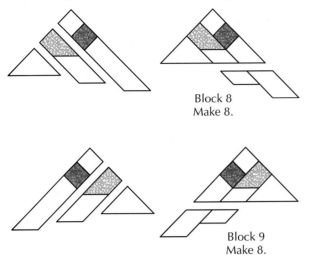

Block 8
Make 8.

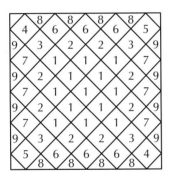

Block 9
Make 8.

5. Referring to the photo on page 17 and the quilt plan below, arrange the blocks, side setting triangles, and corner setting triangles as shown.

6. Sew the blocks together in diagonal rows; press the seams in opposite directions from row to row. Sew the rows together.
7. Layer the quilt top with batting and backing; baste.
8. Quilt as desired or follow the quilting suggestion.
9. Bind the edges, then add a label.

Friendship Baskets

by Sally Schneider, 1997, Mill Creek, Washington, 70" x 70". Sally's small quilt group, the FEQBs, made the blocks. Sally set them together and added three Basket blocks, one with a photo transfer of all six members. The Double Twisted Ribbon border was designed by Janet Inglis. Quilted by Virginia Lauth.

All Night Long

*by Sally Schneider, 1991, Puyallup,
Washington, 76½" x 93½".
Squares with folded corners alternate
with a variation of the Nine Patch
block. Sally made the blocks
while providing nighttime security
for a quilt show at a local mall.
Quilted by Maureen McGee.*

Hovering Hawks

*by Barbara J. Eikmeier, 1997, Fort
Campbell, Kentucky, 45" x 56¼". Fat-
quarter bundles were the inspiration and
source of the fabrics in this wonderful quilt
that is reminiscent of those made in the early
1900s. Barbara chose three prints for each
block: a light, a dark, and a medium.
Each block is different. You may choose
similar assorted prints or use just three prints
for the entire quilt.*

Mosaic

by Barbara J. Eikmeier, 1997, Fort Campbell, Kentucky, 70" x 85". A photo of an Amish quilt provided the color palette for this quilt. Barbara chose an assortment of dark and medium purple and blue prints for her quilt. She made each of the Bachelor's Puzzle blocks with one dark and one medium purple print, or one dark and one medium blue print. The feather plumes quilted in the outer border pay tribute to the Amish inspiration. Collection of Carla Couto.

Quack

*by Sally Schneider, 1991, Puyallup, Washington, 42" x 56". An unusual block found in
Mary Ellen Hopkins' It's OK if You Sit on My Quilt was the start of this gem.
The star in the center of the block forms one of the border units.*

Laurel Wreath

by Barbara J. Eikmeier, 1997, Fort Campbell, Kentucky, 68" x 85". For her twin-size quilt, Barbara purchased two fat-quarter packets to make the Laurel Wreath blocks: a packet of six assorted green prints and a packet of six assorted pink and maroon prints. There are lots of open spaces to show off your hand or machine quilting.

Love in a Mist

by Barbara J. Eikmeier, 1997, Fort Campbell, Kentucky, 42½" x 59½". Barbara also calls this quilt "Do Dogs Go to Heaven?" because she made it during gray January days just after the Eikmeiers' 14-year-old dog died. As Barbara sewed, she reflected on the many years of joy Tanya had given her family. The bright colors and misty borders were a cheerful reminder that helped her decide that, yes, all good dogs must go to heaven.

 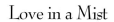

Snail's Trail

by Barbara J. Eikmeier, 1997, Fort Campbell, Kentucky, 70" x 84". Barbara's frequent military moves have taught her to make the best of small quarters. A sewing room always wins out over a guest room, but she dreams of a lovely blue-yellow-and-white guest room. While she dreams, she collects pretty things and makes quilts for the room. She calls this quilt "There's a Guest Room in My Future."

King David's Crown

by Barbara J. Eikmeier, 1997, Fort Campbell, Kentucky, 68" x 85". Two different blocks—King David's Crown and one that forms a chain—combine to create this complex-looking, but easy-to-make quilt. The greens are appropriate for an Army Lieutenant Colonel. Collection of Dale Eikmeier.

Weather Vane

by Barbara J. Eikmeier, 1997, Fort Campbell, Kentucky, 50" x 62½". P&B provided fabric from their Root of All Madder line for this project, which includes thirty-six fabrics from that line. Barbara made nine pairs of blocks, each with a compatible combination of four prints. She used the medium values for the small triangles and house shapes, the dark values for the small squares, and a large floral or striped print for the center square. Medium and dark values formed the "Sawtooth Outie Border." Collection of Sally Schneider.

Finished Block Size: 6"

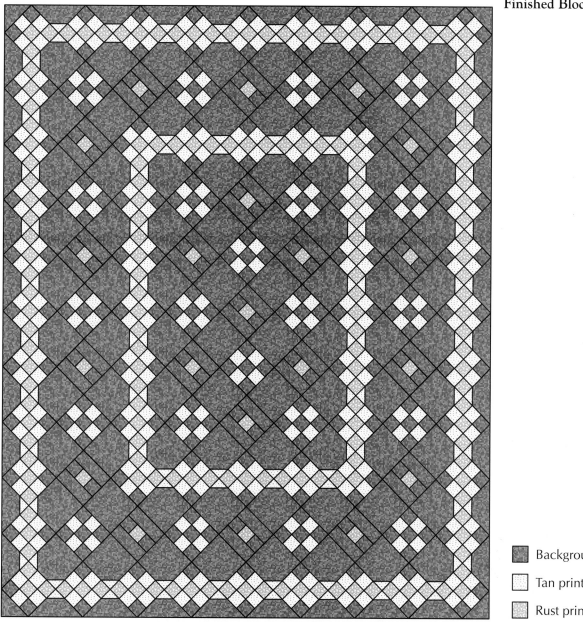

Background

Tan print

Rust print

Materials: 42"-wide fabric		
FABRIC	**QUILT SIZE**	
	LAP 42½" X 51"	TWIN 76½" X 93½"	QUEEN 93½" X 110½"
Background	2¼ yds.	5⅝ yds.	8¼ yds.
Tan print	1⅛ yds.	2⅛ yds.	3 yds.
Rust print	⅝ yd.	1 yd.	1½ yds.
Backing	2¾ yds.	5½ yds.	8¼ yds.
Batting	50" x 60"	85" x 102"	100" x 120"
Binding	½ yd.	¾ yd.	1 yd.

Cutting for Lap Size

Fabric	No. of Strips	Strip Width	No. of Pieces	Piece Size
Background	10	2½"		
	4	6½"	12	2½" x 6½"
			16	6½" x 6½"*
	2	11"	5	11" x 11" ⊠
Tan	14	2½"	36 from 3 strips	2½" x 2½"
Rust	6	2½"		

Cutting for Twin Size

Fabric	No. of Strips	Strip Width	No. of Pieces	Piece Size
Background	19	2½"		
	17	6½"	42	2½" x 6½"
			82	6½" x 6½"*
	3	11"	9	11" x 11" ⊠
Tan	29	2½"	112 from 7 strips	2½" x 2½"
Rust	13	2½"		

Cutting for Queen Size

Fabric	No. of Strips	Strip Width	No. of Pieces	Piece Size
Background	28	2½"		
	24	6½"	70	2½" x 6½"
			120	6½" x 6½"*
	4	11"	11	11" x 11" ⊠
Tan	39	2½"	144 from 9 strips	2½" x 2½"
Rust	17	2½"		

*Cut 2 of these squares once diagonally.

⊠: Cut each square twice diagonally.

Block Assembly

1. Sew the 2½"-wide strips of background, tan, and rust together as shown to create Strip Sets 1, 2, 3, 4, and 5.

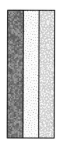 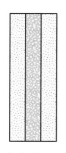 

Strip Set 1
Lap: Make 3.
Twin: Make 7.
Queen: Make 9.

Strip Set 2
Lap: Make 2.
Twin: Make 4.
Queen: Make 5.

Strip Set 3
Lap: Make 1.
Twin: Make 2.
Queen: Make 3.

 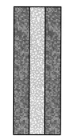

Strip Set 4
Lap: Make 2.
Twin: Make 3.
Queen: Make 5.

Strip Set 5
Lap: Make 1.
Twin: Make 2.
Queen: Make 3.

2. Referring to the chart below, crosscut the strip sets at 2½" intervals into the required number of pieced units.

	LAP	TWIN	QUEEN
Strip Set 1	36	112	144
Strip Set 2	18	56	72
Strip Set 3	12	22	36
Strip Set 4	24	44	72
Strip Set 5	6	21	35

3. Arrange the units as shown and sew them together to complete the Nine Patch blocks.

Block 1
Lap: Make 14.
Twin: Make 48.
Queen: Make 64.

Block 2
Lap: Make 4.
Twin: Make 8.
Queen: Make 8.

Block 3
Lap: Make 12.
Twin: Make 22.
Queen: Make 36.

Block 4
Lap: Make 6.
Twin: Make 21.
Queen: Make 35.

4. Referring to "Making Folded Corners" on page 6, sew 2½" tan squares on the corner (or corners) of 6½" background squares to make Blocks 5 and 6.

Block 5
Lap: Make 10.
Twin: Make 60.
Queen: Make 84.

Block 6
Lap: Make 4.
Twin: Make 8.
Queen: Make 8.

5. Referring to "Making Pieced Edge Triangles" on page 10, sew a 2½" tan square on the top corner of each side setting triangle.

Lap: Make 18.
Twin: Make 36.
Queen: Make 44.

Quilt Top Assembly and Finishing

1. Referring to the photo on page 18 and the quilt plans at right, arrange the blocks, side setting triangles, and corner setting triangles as shown.
2. Sew the blocks together in diagonal rows; press the seams in opposite directions from row to row. Sew the rows together.
3. Layer the quilt top with batting and backing; baste.
4. Quilt as desired or follow the quilting suggestion.
5. Bind the edges, then add a label.

Creative Option
Replace the Block 1 Nine Patch blocks with 6" Ohio Star blocks for another great design.

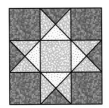

Optional Ohio Star Block

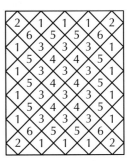

Lap

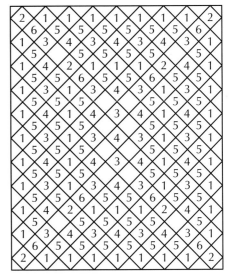

Twin

Queen

Finished Block Size: 10"

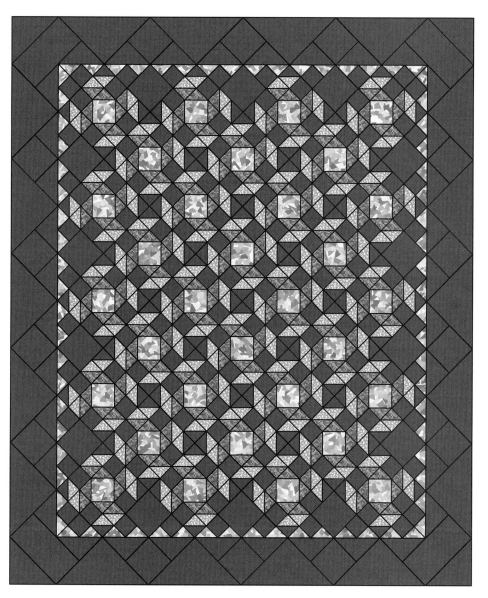

■ Background

▨ Assorted dark prints

▨ Assorted medium prints

▨ Confetti print

Materials: 42"-wide fabric

Fabric	Quilt Size		
	Lap 42½" x 56½"	Twin 70" x 85"	Queen 85" x 99"
Background	3¼ yds.	5¼ yds.	7¾ yds.
Total assorted dark prints	¾ yd.	2¼ yds.	3⅛ yds.
Total assorted medium prints	¾ yd.	2 yds.	3⅛ yds.
Confetti print	¾ yd.	1⅜ yds.	2⅛ yds.
Backing	2¾ yds.	5¼ yds.	8¼ yds.
Batting	48" x 64"	80" x 95"	95" x 108"
Binding	½ yd.	⅝ yd.	¾ yd.

Cutting for Lap Size

Fabric	No. of Strips	Strip Width	No. of Pieces	Piece Size
Background	1	10"	9 wrong side up	2⅝"-wide bias strips
	8	3"	100	3" x 3"
	9	5½"	20	5½" x 5½"
			4	5½" x 10½"
			14	5½" x 6½"
	2	16"	3	16" x 16" ⊠
			2	10" x 10" ◺
Dark	1	10"	9 wrong side up	2⅝"-wide bias strips
	6	3"	72	3" x 3"
Medium	3	10"	18 right side up	2⅝"-wide bias strips
Confetti	3	5½"	18	5½" x 5½"
	3	3"	28	3" x 4"

Cutting for Twin Size

Fabric	No. of Strips	Strip Width	No. of Pieces	Piece Size
Background	3	13"	16 wrong side up	2⅝"-wide bias strips
	13	3"	164	3" x 3"
	8	5½"	28	5½" x 5½"
			4	5½" x 10½"
			18	5½" x 6½"
	3	16"	5	16" x 16" ⊠
			2	10" x 10" ◺
Dark	3	13"	16 wrong side up	2⅝"-wide bias strips
	10	3"	128	3" x 3"
Medium	5	13"	32 right side up	2⅝"-wide bias strips
Confetti	5	5½"	32	5½" x 5½"
	4	3"	36	3" x 4"

◺ : Cut each square once diagonally.
⊠ : Cut each square twice diagonally.

Cutting for Queen Size

Fabric	No. of Strips	Strip Width	No. of Pieces	Piece Size
Background	4	13"	25 wrong side up	2⅝"-wide bias strips
	19	3"	244	3" x 3"
	16	5½"	36	5½" x 5½"
			4	5½" x 10½"
			22	5½" x 6½"
	3	16"	6	16" x 16" ⊠
	1	10"	2	10" x 10" ◻
Dark	4	13"	25 wrong side up	2⅝"-wide bias strips
	16	3"	200	3" x 3"
Medium	8	13"	50 right side up	2⅝"-wide bias strips
Confetti	8	5½"	50	5½" x 5½"
	5	3"	44	3" x 4"

◻ : Cut each square once diagonally.
⊠ : Cut each square twice diagonally.

Block Assembly

1. Referring to the directions for "Making Bias Squares" on page 6, pair 2⅝"-wide bias strips of background and medium prints, right sides together. Sew along both long edges. Cut 3" bias squares from the strips. Press the seams toward the darker fabric.

Quilt Size	Bias-Strip Units	Bias Squares
Lap	9	72
Twin	16	128
Queen	25	200

2. Repeat step 1 with 2⅝"-wide medium and dark bias strips.

Quilt Size	Bias-Strip Units	Bias Squares
Lap	9	72
Twin	16	128
Queen	25	200

3. Referring to "Making Folded Corners" on page 6, sew 3" dark squares on the corners of each 5½" confetti square.

Lap: Make 18.
Twin: Make 32.
Queen: Make 50.

4. Arrange the bias squares from step 1 with 3" background squares and a folded-corner unit as shown. Sew them together to complete Block 1.

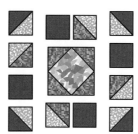
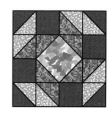

Block 1
Lap: Make 18.
Twin: Make 32.
Queen: Make 50.

Border and Corner Block Assembly

1. Referring to "Making Mary's Triangle Units" on page 8, arrange the 3" x 4" confetti rectangles with 3" background squares as shown and sew them together.

Lap: Make 14.
Twin: Make 18.
Queen: Make 22.

2. To make a template, cut a 5½" square of template material in half diagonally. Draw diagonal lines on the back of the pieced unit from step 1, then place it right sides together with a 5½" x 6½" background rectangle. Sew on the drawn lines, then cut between the lines. Trim the seam allowances to ¼" if desired.

Lap: Make 28.
Twin: Make 36.
Queen: Make 44.

3. Arrange 2 each of the Mary's Triangle units and 5½" background squares as shown. Sew the units together to complete Block 2 for the borders.

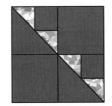

Block 2
Lap: Make 10.
Twin: Make 14.
Queen: Make 18.

4. Arrange 2 Mary's triangle units with a 5½" x 10½" background rectangle as shown. Sew the units together in rows; sew the rows together to complete Block 3 for the corners.

Block 3
All sizes: Make 4.

Quilt Top Assembly and Finishing

1. Referring to the photo on page 19 and the quilt plans below, arrange the blocks, side setting triangles, and corner setting triangles as shown.

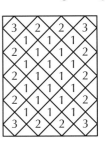

Lap

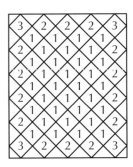

Twin

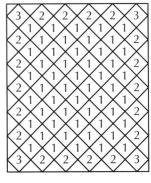

Queen

2. Sew the blocks together in diagonal rows; press the seams in opposite directions from row to row. Sew the rows together.
3. Layer the quilt top with batting and backing; baste.
4. Quilt as desired or follow the quilting suggestion.
5. Bind the edges, then add a label.

Cutting for Queen Size

Fabric	No. of Strips	Strip Width	No. of Pieces	Piece Size
Background	2	11"	14 wrong side up	2¼"-wide bias strips
	9	8½"	35	8½" x 8½"
	3	4½"	24	4½" x 4½"
	4	2½"	56	2½" x 2½"
Light	3	11"	24 wrong side up	2¼"-wide bias strips
	7	4½"	48	4½" x 5½"
	6	2½"	96	2½" x 2½"
Dark	5	11"	36 right side up	2¼"-wide bias strips
	6	3½"	96	2½" x 3½"
Medium	2	11"	12 wrong side up	2¼"-wide bias strips
	6	2½"	96	2½" x 2½"
Dark red	3	11"	21 right side up	2¼"-wide bias strips
	4	2½"	60	2½" x 2½"
Navy blue	4	4½"	32	4½" x 4½"
	1	11"	7 wrong side up	2¼"-wide bias strips
	4	14"	7	14" x 14" ⊠
			2	8" x 8" ◹

◹ : Cut each square once diagonally.

⊠ : Cut each square twice diagonally. Lap and queen sizes will have 2 extra.

Block Assembly

1. Referring to "Making Bias Squares" on page 6, pair 2¼"-wide bias strips of light and dark prints, right sides together. Sew along both long edges. Cut 2½" bias squares from the strips. Press the seams toward the dark fabric.

Quilt Size	Bias-Strip Units	Bias Squares
Lap	6	48
Twin	12	96
Queen	24	192

2. Repeat step 1 with 2¼"-wide bias strips of dark and medium prints.

Quilt Size	Bias-Strip Units	Bias Squares
Lap	3	24
Twin	6	48
Queen	12	96

3. Referring to "Making Mary's Triangle Units" on page 8, arrange 2 dark/medium bias squares with 2 dark rectangles, each 2½" x 3½". Sew them together as shown. Clip the center seam, then press the seam allowances toward the rectangles.

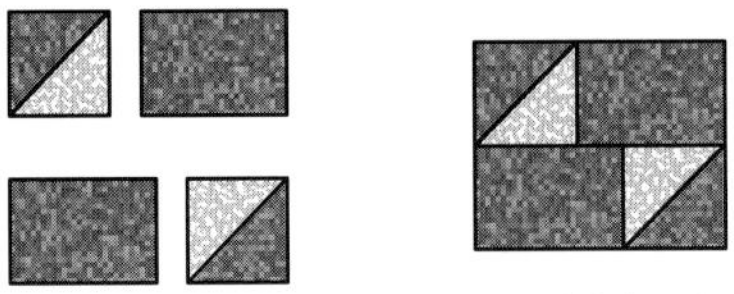

Lap: Make 12.
Twin: Make 24.
Queen: Make 48.

4. To make a template, cut a 4½" square of template material in half diagonally. Draw diagonal lines on the wrong side of the pieced unit from step 3, then place it right sides together with a 4½" x 5½" light rectangle. Sew on the drawn lines, then cut between the lines. Trim the seam allowances to ¼" if desired.

Lap: Make 24.
Twin: Make 48.
Queen: Make 96.

5. Arrange 2 dark/light bias squares with a 2½" medium square and a 2½" light square. Sew them together to complete the bias-square unit.

 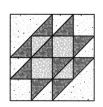

Lap: Make 24.
Twin: Make 48.
Queen: Make 96.

6. Arrange 2 Mary's Triangle units and 2 bias-square units as shown. Sew them together to complete Block 1, the Hovering Hawks block.

Block 1
Lap: Make 12.
Twin: Make 24.
Queen: Make 48.

Border and Corner Block Assembly

1. Pair 2¼"-wide bias strips of background and dark red, right sides together. Sew along both long edges. Cut 2½" bias squares from the strips. Press the seams toward the darker fabric.

Quilt Size	Bias-Strip Units	Bias Squares
Lap	9	56
Twin	10	80
Queen	14	112

2. Repeat step 1 with 2¼"-wide bias strips of dark red and navy blue.

Quilt Size	Bias-Strip Units	Bias Squares
Lap	4	28
Twin	5	40
Queen	7	56

3. Referring to "Making Folded Corners" on page 6, sew a 2½" dark red square on 1 corner of each 4½" navy blue border square. Press half toward the triangle and half toward the square. Reserve 8 for Block 3.

Lap: Make 18.
Twin: Make 24.
Queen: Make 32.

4. Arrange 2 background/dark red bias squares with 1 dark red/navy blue bias square and 1 background 2½" square as shown. Sew them together to complete the bias-square section. Reserve 8 for Block 3.

Lap: Make 28.
Twin: Make 40.
Queen: Make 56.

5. Arrange the folded-corner unit, bias-square sections, and background square as shown, then sew them together to complete Block 2 for the borders.

 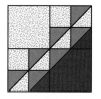

Block 2
Lap: Make 10.
Twin: Make 16.
Queen: Make 24.

6. Arrange the folded-corner units and bias-square sections as shown, then sew them together to complete Block 3 for the corners.

Block 3
All sizes: Make 4.

Quilt Top Assembly and Finishing

1. Referring to "Making Pieced Edge Triangles" on page 10, sew a 2½" red square on the top corner of each side setting triangle.

Lap: Make 14.
Twin: Make 20.
Queen: Make 28.

2. Referring to the photo on page 18 and the quilt plans below, arrange the blocks, side setting triangles, and corner setting triangles as shown.

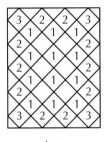

Lap

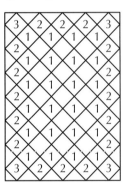

Twin

3. Sew the blocks together in diagonal rows; press the seams in opposite directions from row to row. Sew the rows together.
4. Layer the quilt top with batting and backing; baste.
5. Quilt as desired or follow the quilting suggestion.
6. Bind the edges, then add a label.

Queen

King David's Crown

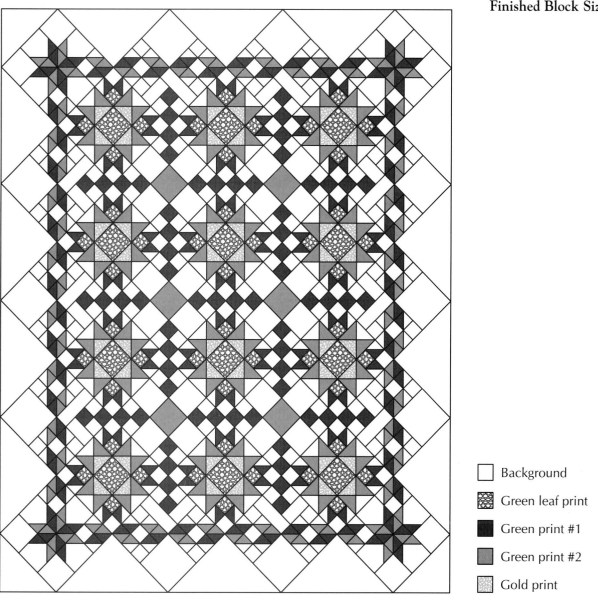

- ☐ Background
- ▨ Green leaf print
- ■ Green print #1
- ▨ Green print #2
- ▨ Gold print

Materials: 42"-wide fabric

FABRIC	QUILT SIZE		
	LAP 51" X 68"	TWIN 68" X 85"	QUEEN 85" X 102"
Background	3⅝ yds.	5½ yds.	7⅞ yds.
Green leaf print	½ yd.	½ yd.	⅞ yd.
Green print #1	1⅜ yds.	2 yds.	2¾ yds.
Green print #2	1⅛ yds.	2 yds.	3 yds.
Gold print	½ yd.	½ yd.	¾ yd.
Backing	3¼ yds.	5⅛ yds.	7⅞ yds.
Batting	57" x 74"	74" x 91"	91" x 110"
Binding	½ yd.	⅝ yd.	¾ yd.

Cutting for Lap Size

Fabric	No. of Strips	Strip Width	No. of Pieces	Piece Size
Background	2	12"	14 right side up	2¼"-wide bias strips
			3 right side up	3⅞"-wide bias strips
	1	6½"	6	6½" x 6½"
	3	4½"	32	4½" x 4½"
	9	2½"	68 from 5 strips	2½" x 2½"
	2	19"	3	19" x 19" ⊠
	1	12"	2	12" x 12" ◺
Leaf print	1	4½"	6	4½" x 4½"
	2	2½"	24	2½" x 2½"
Green print #1	3	12"	10 wrong side up	2¼"-wide bias strips
			6 right side up	2¼"-wide bias strips
	3	2½"	16 from 1 strip	2½" x 2½"
Green print #2	2	12"	10 wrong side up	2¼"-wide bias strips
			6 wrong side up	3⅞"-wide bias strips
	1	4½"	2	4½" x 4½"
	1	2½"	16	2½" x 2½"
Gold print	1	12"	3 right side up	3⅞"-wide bias strips

Cutting for Twin Size

Fabric	No. of Strips	Strip Width	No. of Pieces	Piece Size
Background	4	12"	24 right side up	2¼"-wide bias strips
			6 right side up	3⅞"-wide bias strips
	2	6½"	10	6½" x 6½"
	6	4½"	48	4½" x 4½"
	15	2½"	116 from 8 strips	2½" x 2½"
	2	19"	4	19" x 19" ⊠
	1	12"	2	12" x 12" ◺
Leaf print	1	4½"	12	4½" x 4½"
	3	2½"	48	2½" x 2½"
Green print #1	4	12"	18 wrong side up	2¼"-wide bias strips
			8 right side up	2¼"-wide bias strips
	6	2½"	16 from 1 strip	2½" x 2½"
Green print #2	4	12"	14 wrong side up	2¼"-wide bias strips
			12 wrong side up	3⅞"-wide bias strips
	2	4½"	6	4½" x 4½"
	2	2½"	16	2½" x 2½"
Gold print	1	12"	6 right side up	3⅞"-wide bias strips

◺ : Cut each square once diagonally.

⊠ : Cut each square twice diagonally. There will be 2 extra triangles for each size.

Cutting for Queen Size

Fabric	No. of Strips	Strip Width	No. of Pieces	Piece Size
Background	6	12"	36 right side up	2¼"-wide bias strips
			10 right side up	3⅞"-wide bias strips
	3	6½"	14	6½" x 6½"
	8	4½"	72	4½" x 4½"
	24	2½"	172 from 11 strips	2½" x 2½"
	3	19"	5	19" x 19" ⊠
	1	12"	2	12" x 12" ◺
Leaf print	3	4½"	20	4½" x 4½"
	5	2½"	80	2½" x 2½"
Green print #1	6	12"	28 wrong side up	2¼"-wide bias strips
			10 right side up	2¼"-wide bias strips
	9	2½"	16 from 1 strip	2½" x 2½"
Green print #2	7	12"	18 wrong side up	2¼"-wide bias strips
			20 wrong side up	3⅞"-wide bias strips
	2	4½"	12	4½" x 4½"
	1	2½"	16	2½" x 2½"
Gold print	2	12"	10 right side up	3⅞"-wide bias strips

◺: Cut each square once diagonally.

⊠: Cut each square twice diagonally. There will be 2 extra triangles for each size.

Block Assembly

1. Referring to "Making Bias Squares" on page 6, pair 2¼"-wide bias strips of green print #1 and background, right sides together. Sew along both long edges. Cut 2½" bias squares from the strips. Press the seams toward the darker fabric.

Quilt Size	Bias-Strip Units	Bias Squares
Lap	10	80
Twin	18	144
Queen	28	224

2. Repeat step 1 with 3⅞"-wide bias strips of green print #2 and background; repeat with 3⅞"-wide bias strips of green print #2 and gold print. Cut 4⅞" bias squares from the strips. (Numbers of bias-strip units and bias squares to cut are for each combination.) Press the seams toward green print #2.

Quilt Size	Bias-Strip Units	Bias Squares
Lap	3	12
Twin	6	24
Queen	10	40

3. Referring to "Making Quarter-Square Triangle Units" on page 8, place 1 each of the bias squares made in step 2 right sides together as shown. On the wrong side of 1 bias square, draw a diagonal line from corner to corner, crossing the seam line. Sew ¼" from each side of the line. Cut on the drawn line to complete the quarter-square triangle units.

Lap: Make 24.
Twin: Make 48.
Queen: Make 80.

4. Arrange 2 bias squares from step 1 with a 2½" leaf print square and a 2½" background square as shown; sew them together to make the corner units. Reserve the remaining bias squares for Blocks 3 and 4.

Lap: Make 24.
Twin: Make 48.
Queen: Make 80.

5. Arrange 4 corner units, 4 quarter-square triangle units, and 1 leaf-print square, 4½" x 4½", as shown. Sew them together to complete Block 1, the King David's Crown block.

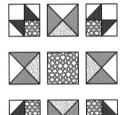 

Block 1
Lap: Make 6.
Twin: Make 12.
Queen: Make 20.

6. Sew a 2½"-wide green print #1 strip to a 2½"-wide background strip. Press the seam toward the dark fabric. Crosscut the strip set at 2½" intervals. Sew the segments together to make four-patch units.

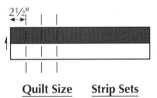

Quilt Size	Strip Sets
Lap	2
Twin	5
Queen	8

Four-Patch Unit
Lap: Make 14.
Twin: Make 34.
Queen: Make 62.

7. Arrange 4 four-patch units with a 4½" green print #2 square and 4 background 4½" squares as shown. Sew them together to complete Block 2. Reserve the remaining four-patch units and background squares for the side and corner border blocks.

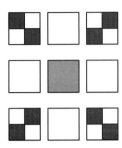 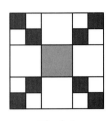

Block 2
Lap: Make 2.
Twin: Make 6.
Queen: Make 12.

Border and Corner Block Assembly

1. Pair 2¼"-wide bias strips of green print #2 and background, right sides together. Sew along both long edges. Cut 2½" bias squares from the strips. Press the seams toward the darker fabric.

Quilt Size	Bias-Strip Units	Bias Squares
Lap	4	32
Twin	6	48
Queen	8	64

2. Repeat step 1 with 2¼"-wide bias strips of green print #1 and green print #2. Cut 2½" bias squares from the strips. Press the seams toward the darker fabric.

Quilt Size	Bias-Strip Units	Bias Squares
Lap	6	48
Twin	8	64
Queen	10	80

3. Referring to "Making Folded Corners" on page 6, sew a 2½" green print #2 square to the bottom left corner of a 4½" background square. Sew a 2½" green print #1 square to the right corner.

All sizes: Make 16.

4. Stitch the reserved four-patch units to a 2½" background strip. Position the four-patch units as close together as possible without overlapping the edges. Make sure the four-patch units are in the proper position. Cut the units apart, trimming away any excess fabric between them. Press the seams toward the background strip.

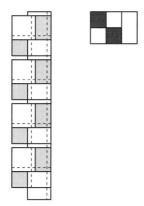

5. Stitch the units completed in step 4 to another 2½" background strip. Position them as close together as possible without overlapping the edges. Cut them apart, trimming away any excess fabric between them. Press the seams toward the background strip.

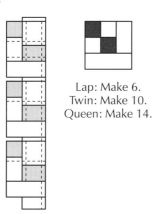

Lap: Make 6.
Twin: Make 10.
Queen: Make 14.

6. Arrange the 2½" bias squares and background squares as shown, then sew them together.

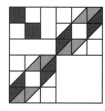

Lap: Make 12.
Twin: Make 20.
Queen: Make 28.

7. Arrange the units from steps 5 and 6 with a 6½" background square as shown. Sew them together to complete Block 3 for the side borders.

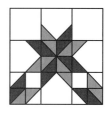

Block 3
Lap: Make 6.
Twin: Make 10.
Queen: Make 14.

8. Arrange the bias squares with the folded-corner units and background squares as shown. Sew them together to complete Block 4 for the border corner blocks.

Block 4
All sizes: Make 4.

Quilt Top Assembly and Finishing

1. Referring to the photo on page 23 and the quilt plans below, arrange the blocks, side setting triangles, and corner setting triangles as shown.

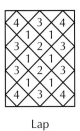

Lap

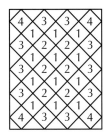

Twin

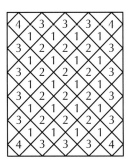

Queen

2. Sew the blocks together in diagonal rows; press the seams in opposite directions from row to row. Sew the rows together.
3. Layer the quilt top with batting and backing; baste.
4. Quilt as desired or follow the quilting suggestion.
5. Bind the edges, then add a label.

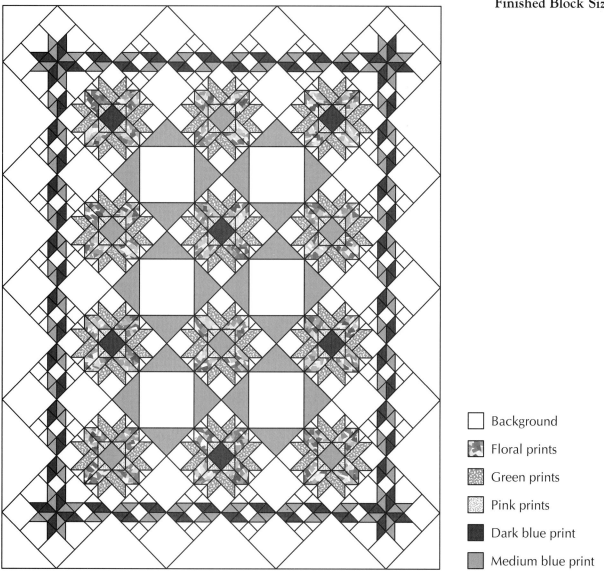

	Background
	Floral prints
	Green prints
	Pink prints
	Dark blue print
	Medium blue print

Materials: 42"-wide fabric			
FABRIC	**QUILT SIZE**		
	LAP 51" X 68"	TWIN 68" X 85"	QUEEN 85" X 102"
Background	4 yds.	5⅝ yds.	8 yds.
Floral prints	⅛ yd. each of 6	⅛ yd. each of 12	⅛ yd. each of 20
Assorted green prints	⅝ yd.	⅞ yd.	1⅛ yds.
Assorted pink prints	¼ yd.	⅜ yd.	⅝ yd.
Dark blue print	⅞ yd.	1 yd.	1⅝ yds.
Medium blue print	1¼ yds.	1⅝ yds.	2⅜ yds.
Backing	3¼ yds.	5¼ yds.	7⅞ yds.
Batting	56" x 73"	73" x 90"	90" x 108"
Binding	½ yd.	⅝ yd.	¾ yd.

Cutting for Lap Size

Fabric	No. of Strips	Strip Width	No. of Pieces	Piece Size
Background	2	12"	4 right side up	2¼"-wide bias strips
			4 wrong side up	2¼"-wide bias strips
			2	12" x 12" ◹
	5	2"	96	2" x 2"
	3	3½"	24	3½" x 3½"
	3	2½"	44	2½" x 2½"
	2	6½"	12	6½" x 6½"
	3	4½"	24	4½" x 4½"
	1	9"	2	9" x 9"
	2	19"	3	19" x 19" ⊠
Each floral print	1	2"	8**	2" x 5"
Green	2	5"	24*	2" x 5"
	2	3½"	24*	2" x 3½"
Pink	3	2"	48**	2" x 2"
Dark blue	1	3½"	3	3½" x 3½"
	2	12"	10 wrong side up	2¼" bias strips
	1	2½"	16	2½" x 2½"
Medium blue	1	3½"	3	3½" x 3½"
	2	12"	10 right side up	2¼" bias strips
	1	6⅞"	4	6⅞" x 6⅞"
	1	2½"	16	2½" x 2½"

Cutting for Twin Size

Fabric	No. of Strips	Strip Width	No. of Pieces	Piece Size
Background	3	12"	6 right side up	2¼"-wide bias strips
			6 wrong side up	2¼"-wide bias strips
			2	12" x 12" ◹
	10	2"	192	2" x 2"
	5	3½"	48	3½" x 3½"
	5	2½"	68	2½" x 2½"
	4	6½"	20	6½" x 6½"
	4	4½"	24	4½" x 4½"
	2	9"	6	9" x 9"
	2	19"	4	19" x 19" ⊠
Each floral print	1	2"	8**	2" x 5"

*Cut 4 of these rectangles from one print for each block.

**Cut 8 of these squares or rectangles from one print for each block.

◹: Cut each square once diagonally.

⊠: Cut each square twice diagonally.

Cutting for Twin Size continued

Fabric	No. of Strips	Strip Width	No. of Pieces	Piece Size
Green	3	5"	48*	2" x 5"
	3	3½"	48*	2" x 3½"
Pink	5	2"	96**	2" x 2"
Dark blue	1	3½"	6	3½" x 3½"
	2	12"	14 wrong side up	2¼"-wide bias strips
	1	2½"	16	2½" x 2½"
Medium blue	1	3½"	6	3½" x 3½"
	2	12"	14 right side up	2¼"-wide bias strips
	3	6⅞"	12	6⅞" x 6⅞"
	1	2½"	16	2½" x 2½"

Cutting for Queen Size

Fabric	No. of Strips	Strip Width	No. of Pieces	Piece Size
Background	3	12"	8 right side up	2¼"-wide bias strips
			8 wrong side up	2¼"-wide bias strips
			2 from 1 strip	12" x 12" ◻
	16	2"	320	2" x 2"
	8	3½"	80	3½" x 3½"
	6	2½"	92	2½" x 2½"
	5	6½"	28	6½" x 6½"
	3	4½"	24	4½" x 4½"
	3	9"	12	9" x 9"
	3	19"	5	19" x 19" ⊠
Each floral print	1	2"	8**	2" x 5"
Green	4	5"	80*	2" x 5"
	4	3½"	80*	2" x 3½"
Pink	8	2"	160**	2" x 2"
Dark blue	1	3½"	10	3½" x 3½"
	3	12"	18 wrong side up	2¼"-wide bias strips
	1	2½"	16	2½" x 2½"
Medium blue	1	3½"	10	3½" x 3½"
	3	12"	18 right side up	2¼"-wide bias strips
	5	6⅞"	24	6⅞" x 6⅞"
	1	2½"	16	2½" x 2½"

*Cut 4 of these rectangles from one print for each block.
**Cut 8 of these squares or rectangles from one print for each block.
◻: Cut each square once diagonally.
⊠: Cut each square twice diagonally.

Quilt Top Assembly and Finishing

1. Referring to the photo on page 21 and the quilt plans below, arrange the blocks, side setting triangles, and corner setting triangles as shown.

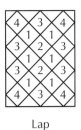

Lap

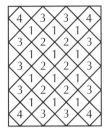

Twin

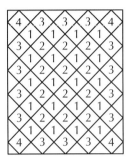

Queen

2. Sew the blocks together in diagonal rows; press the seams in opposite directions from row to row. Sew the rows together.
3. Layer the quilt top with batting and backing; baste.
4. Quilt as desired or follow the quilting suggestion.
5. Bind the edges, then add a label.

Love in a Mist

- ☐ Background
- ☐ Yellow print
- ☐ Green print
- ☐ Light blue print
- ☐ Dark blue print
- ☐ Rainbow print

Materials: 42"-wide fabric			
Fabric	**Quilt Size**		
	Lap 42½" x 59½"	Twin 59½" x 76½"	Queen 93½" x 93½"
Background	1¾ yds.	3¼ yds.	6 yds.
Yellow print	½ yd.	¾ yd.	1½ yds.
Green print	½ yd.	¾ yd.	1½ yds.
Light blue print	⅝ yd.	¾ yd.	1⅝ yds.
Dark blue print	¾ yd.	1⅜ yds.	2½ yds.
Rainbow print	2⅛ yds.	3 yds.	4⅞ yds.
Backing	2¾ yds.	3⅝ yds.	8¼ yds.
Batting	49" x 66"	66" x 83"	100" x 100"
Binding	½ yd.	⅝ yd.	¾ yd.

Cutting for Lap Size

Fabric	No. of Strips	Strip Width	No. of Pieces	Piece Size
Background	2	12"	13 right side up	2¼"-wide bias strips
	6	2½"	96	2½" x 2½"
	3	4½"	20	4½" x 4½"
	1	6½"	6	6½" x 6½"
Yellow	1	12"	4 wrong side up	2¼"-wide bias strips
			4 right side up	2¼"-wide bias strips
Green	1	12"	8 wrong side up	2¼"-wide bias strips
Light blue	1	12"	4 right side up	2¼"-wide bias strips
	2	2½"	32	2½" x 2½"
Dark blue	1	12"	9 wrong side up	2¼"-wide bias strips
	4	2½"	52	2½" x 2½"
Rainbow	5	4½"	32	4½" x 4½"
			20	2½" x 4½"
	2	2½"	20	2½" x 2½"
	2	11"	6	11" x 11" ⊠
	1	12"	2	12" x 12" ◻

Cutting for Twin Size

Fabric	No. of Strips	Strip Width	No. of Pieces	Piece Size
Background	3	12"	25 right side up	2¼"-wide bias strips
	14	2½"	216	2½" x 2½"
	4	4½"	28	4½" x 4½"
	2	6½"	10	6½" x 6½"
Yellow	2	12"	9 wrong side up	2¼"-wide bias strips
			9 right side up	2¼"-wide bias strips
Green	2	12"	18 wrong side up	2¼"-wide bias strips
Light blue	1	12"	9 right side up	2¼"-wide bias strips
	5	2½"	72	2½" x 2½"
Dark blue	2	12"	16 wrong side up	2¼"-wide bias strips
	7	2½"	100	2½" x 2½"
Rainbow	10	4½"	72	4½" x 4½"
			28	2½" x 4½"
	2	2½"	28	2½" x 2½"
	3	11"	8	11" x 11" ⊠
	1	12"	2	12" x 12" ◻

◻ : Cut each square once diagonally.

⊠ : Cut each square twice diagonally.

Cutting for Queen Size

Fabric	No. of Strips	Strip Width	No. of Pieces	Piece Size
Background	6	12"	52 right side up	2¼"-wide bias strips
	31	2½"	492	2½" x 2½"
	5	4½"	40	4½" x 4½"
	3	6½"	16	6½" x 6½"
Yellow	4	12"	21 wrong side up	2¼"-wide bias strips
			21 right side up	2¼"-wide bias strips
Green	4	12"	42 wrong side up	2¼"-wide bias strips
Light blue	2	12"	21 right side up	2¼"-wide bias strips
	11	2½"	164	2½" x 2½"
Dark blue	4	12"	31 wrong side up	2¼"-wide bias strips
	13	2½"	204	2½" x 2½"
Rainbow	21	4½"	164	4½" x 4½"
			40	2½" x 4½"
	3	2½"	40	2½" x 2½"
	4	11"	11	11" x 11" ⊠
	1	12"	2	12" x 12" ◹

◹ : Cut each square once diagonally.
⊠ : Cut each square twice diagonally.

Block Assembly

1. Referring to "Making Bias Squares" on page 6, pair 2¼"-wide bias strips of background and yellow, right sides together. Sew along both long edges. Cut 2½" bias squares from the strips. Press the seams toward the darker fabric.

Quilt Size	Bias-Strip Units	Bias Squares
Lap	4	32
Twin	9	72
Queen	21	164

2. Repeat step 1 with 2¼"-wide green and yellow bias strips.

Quilt Size	Bias-Strip Units	Bias Squares
Lap	4	32
Twin	9	72
Queen	21	164

3. Repeat step 1 with 2¼"-wide green and background bias strips.

Quilt Size	Bias-Strip Units	Bias Squares
Lap	4	32
Twin	9	72
Queen	21	164

4. Repeat step 1 with 2¼"-wide light blue and dark blue bias strips.

Quilt Size	Bias-Strip Units	Bias Squares
Lap	4	32
Twin	9	72
Queen	21	164

5. Referring to "Making Folded Corners" on page 6, sew a dark blue 2½" square on the lower left corner of each 4½" rainbow square. Sew a 2½" light blue square on the lower right corner; stitch 2½" background squares on the 2 remaining corners.

Lap: Make 32.
Twin: Make 72.
Queen: Make 164.

6. Arrange a 2½" background square with 3 appropriately colored bias squares as shown. Sew them together to create the block-corner units.

Lap: Make 32.
Twin: Make 72.
Queen: Make 164.

7. Arrange the dark blue and light blue bias squares as shown, then sew them together to create the block centers.

Lap: Make 8.
Twin: Make 18.
Queen: Make 41.

8. Arrange 4 folded-corner units, 4 block-corner units, and 1 block center as shown to complete Block 1, the Love in a Mist block.

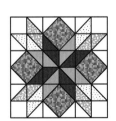

Block 1
Lap: Make 8.
Twin: Make 18.
Queen: Make 41.

Border and Corner Block Assembly

1. Pair 2¼"-wide bias strips of background and dark blue, right sides together. Sew along both long edges. Cut 2½" bias squares from the strips. Press the seams toward the darker fabric.

Quilt Size	Bias-Strip Units	Bias Squares
Lap	5	40
Twin	7	56
Queen	10	80

2. Using the folded-corner technique, sew a 2½" dark blue square on 1 corner of each 4½" background square.

Lap: Make 20.
Twin: Make 28.
Queen: Make 40.

3. Arrange a folded-corner unit with 2 dark blue/background bias squares, a 2½" rainbow square, and a 2½" x 4½" rainbow rectangle as shown; sew them together.

Lap: Make 20.
Twin: Make 28.
Queen: Make 40.

4. Arrange 2 units from step 3, 1 rainbow side setting triangle, and 1 background 6½" square as shown; sew them together to create Block 2.

Block 2
Lap: Make 6.
Twin: Make 10.
Queen: Make 16.

5. Arrange 2 units from step 3 and a corner setting triangle as shown; sew them together to create Block 3.

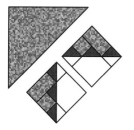
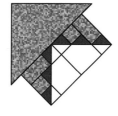

Block 3
All sizes: Make 4.

Quilt Top Assembly and Finishing

1. Referring to the photo on page 21 and the quilt plans below, arrange the blocks and side setting triangles as shown.

Lap

Twin

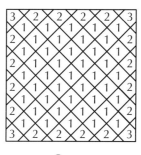

Queen

2. Sew the blocks together in diagonal rows; press the seams in opposite directions from row to row. Sew the rows together.

3. Layer the quilt top with batting and backing; baste.
4. Quilt as desired or follow the quilting suggestion.
5. Bind the edges, then add a label.

Tip

The seams joining the outer border blocks must match perfectly so the triangle border forms a straight line. If they do not, take a slightly deeper seam (just a few threads) at the mismatched spot; that usually brings the points into line.

-------- Original seam
-------- Adjusted seam

Quack

Finished Block Size: 10"

- ☐ Background
- ■ Dark blue prints
- ▦ Light blue prints
- ▨ Burgundy prints
- ▦ Floral print

Materials: 42"-wide fabric

Fabric	Quilt Size		
	LAP 42" x 56"	TWIN 71" x 99"	QUEEN 85" x 99"
Background	2¼ yds.	6 yds.	7½ yds.
Dark blue prints	⅞ yd.	2½ yds.	3½ yds.
Light blue prints	⅝ yd.	1½ yds.	2 yds.
Burgundy prints	¼ yd.	⅜ yd.	⅜ yd.
Floral print	1⅝ yds.	2¼ yds.	2⅝ yds.
Backing	2¾ yds.	6 yds.	7¾ yds.
Batting	50" x 64"	79" x 108"	93" x 108"
Binding	½ yd.	¾ yd.	¾ yd.

Cutting for Lap Size

Fabric	No. of Strips	Strip Width	No. of Pieces	Piece Size
Background	2	12"	13 right side up	2¼"-wide bias strips
	3	6½"	36	2½" x 6½"
	2	4½"	10	4½" x 4½"
			12	2½" x 4½"
	7	2½"	6	2½" x 8½"
			66	2½" x 2½"
Dark blue	6	2½"	94	2½" x 2½"
Light blue	1	12"	5 wrong side up	2¼"-wide bias strips
	3	2½"	40	2½" x 2½"
Burgundy	1	12"	5 wrong side up	2¼"-wide bias strips
	2	2½"	20	2½" x 2½"
Floral	1	12"	3 wrong side up	2¼"-wide bias strips
	2	4½"	14	4½" x 4½"
	2	16"	3	16" x 16" ⊠
			2	10" x 10" ◺

Cutting for Twin Size

Fabric	No. of Strips	Strip Width	No. of Pieces	Piece Size
Background	5	12"	35 right side up	2¼"-wide bias strips
	10	6½"	160	2½" x 6½"
	5	4½"	20	4½" x 4½"
			32	2½" x 4½"
	17	2½"	16	2½" x 8½"
			220	2½" x 2½"
Dark blue	24	2½"	372	2½" x 2½"
Light blue	1	12"	10	2¼"-wide bias strips
	13	2½"	195	2½" x 2½"
Burgundy	2	12"	20 wrong side up	2¼"-wide bias strips
	3	2½"	40	2½" x 2½"
Floral	1	12"	5 wrong side up	2¼"-wide bias strips
	3	4½"	24	4½" x 4½"
	3	16"	5	16" x 16" ⊠
			2	10" x 10" ◺

◺: Cut each square once diagonally.
⊠: Cut each square twice diagonally.

Cutting for Queen Size

Fabric	No. of Strips	Strip Width	No. of Pieces	Piece Size
Background	6	12"	42 right side up	2¼"-wide bias strips
	14	6½"	204	2½" x 6½"
	6	4½"	22	4½" x 4½"
			36	2½" x 4½"
	21	2½"	18	2½" x 8½"
			270	2½" x 2½"
Dark blue	30	2½"	466	2½" x 2½"
Light blue	2	12"	11 wrong side up	2¼"-wide bias strips
	16	2½"	250	2½" x 2½"
Burgundy	3	12"	25 wrong side up	2¼"-wide bias strips
	3	2½"	44	2½" x 2½"
Floral	1	12"	6 wrong side up	2¼"-wide bias strips
	3	4½"	26	4½" x 4½"
	3	16"	6	16" x 16" ⊠
	1	10"	2	10" x 10" ◹

◹ : Cut each square once diagonally.

⊠ : Cut each square twice diagonally.

Block Assembly

1. Referring to "Making Bias Squares" on page 6, pair 2¼"-wide bias strips of background and burgundy, right sides together. Sew along both long edges. Cut 2½" bias squares from the strips. Press the seams toward the darker fabric.

Quilt Size	Bias-Strip Units	Bias Squares
Lap	5	32
Twin	20	156
Queen	25	200

2. Reserve 4 rectangles, each 2½" x 6½", for Block 3. Referring to "Making Folded Corners" on page 6, sew a dark blue 2½" square on each end of a 2½" x 6½" background rectangle in the direction shown.

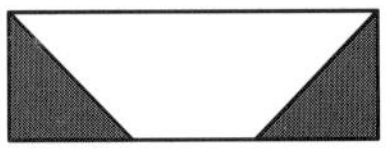

Lap: Make 32.
Twin: Make 156.
Queen: Make 200.

3. Arrange the burgundy/background bias squares with the 2½" light blue and background squares and the folded-corner units as shown. Sew the units together in rows. Sew the rows together to complete Block 1.

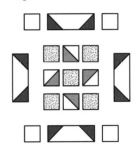

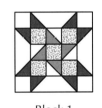

Block 1
Lap: Make 8.
Twin: Make 39.
Queen: Make 50.

Border and Corner Block Assembly

1. Pair 2¼"-wide bias strips of light blue and background, right sides together. Sew along both long edges. Cut 2½" bias squares from the strips. Press the seams toward the darker fabric.

Quilt Size	Bias-Strip Units	Bias Squares
Lap	5	40
Twin	10	80
Queen	11	88

2. Repeat step 1 with 2¼"-wide floral and background strips.

Quilt Size	Bias-Strip Units	Bias Squares
Lap	3	20
Twin	5	40
Queen	6	44

3. Using the folded-corner technique, sew a 2½" background square on one corner of each 4½" floral print square.

Lap: Make 14.
Twin: Make 24.
Queen: Make 26.

4. Arrange the units from steps 1–3 with the 2½" burgundy, dark blue, and background squares plus the 2½" x 4½" and 2½" x 8½" rectangles as shown; sew them together to complete Block 2.

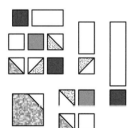

Block 2
Lap: Make 6.
Twin: Make 16.
Queen: Make 18.

5. From each of the leftover background and floral fabrics, cut 1 square, 3¼" x 3¼". From the floral fabric, cut 2 squares, each 2⅞" x 2⅞". Referring to "Making Quarter-Square Triangle Units" on page 8, make 4 quarter-square triangle units.

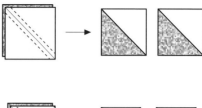

All sizes: Make 4.

6. Arrange the quarter-square triangle units with the remaining squares, rectangles, and bias squares as shown; sew them together to complete Block 3.

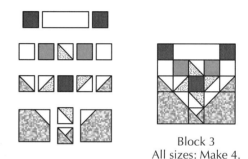

Block 3
All sizes: Make 4.

Quilt Top Assembly and Finishing

1. Referring to "Making Pieced Edge Triangles" on page 10, sew a 4½" background square on the tip of each side setting triangle.

Lap: Make 10.
Twin: Make 20.
Queen: Make 22.

2. Referring to the photo on page 20 and the quilt plans below, arrange the blocks, side setting triangles, and corner setting triangles as shown.

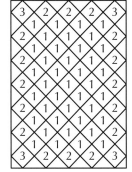

Lap

Twin

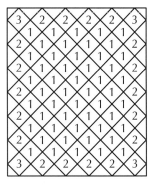

Queen

3. Sew the blocks together in diagonal rows; press the seams in opposite directions from row to row. Sew the rows together.
4. Layer the quilt top with batting and backing; baste.
5. Quilt as desired or follow the quilting suggestion.
6. Bind the edges, then add a label.

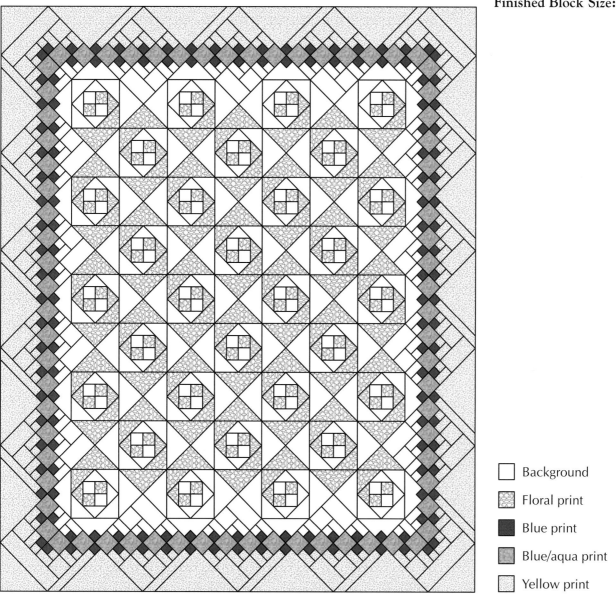

Background
Floral print
Blue print
Blue/aqua print
Yellow print

FABRIC	QUILT SIZE		
	LAP 56" x 70"	TWIN 70" x 84"	QUEEN 84" x 96"
Background	2⅜ yds.	3¼ yds.	5 yds.
Floral print	1⅞ yds.	2⅛ yds.	3⅜ yds.
Blue print	½ yd.	⅝ yd.	¾ yd.
Blue/aqua print	⅝ yd.	⅝ yd.	¾ yd.
Yellow print	2⅛ yds.	2½ yds.	3 yds.
Backing	3½ yds.	5 yds.	7½ yds.
Batting	62" x 76"	76" x 90"	90" x 102"
Binding	½ yd.	⅝ yd.	¾ yd.

Materials: 42"-wide fabric

Cutting for Lap Size

Fabric	No. of Strips	Strip Width	No. of Pieces	Piece Size
Background	4	5⅞"	21	5⅞" x 5⅞"
	3	4⅜"	21	4⅜" x 4⅜"
	2	3⅜"	21	3⅜" x 3⅜"
	3	2¼"		
	3	3"	10	3" x 3"
			10	3" x 5½"
	7	1¾"		
Floral	3	5⅞"	15	5⅞" x 5⅞"
	3	4⅜"	15	4⅜" x 4⅜"
	2	3⅜"	15	3⅜" x 3⅜"
	3	2¼"		
Blue	8	1¾"	28 from 2 strips	1¾" x 1¾"
Blue/aqua	5	3"	56	3" x 3"
Yellow	7	1¾"		
	4	3"	18	3" x 3"
			10	3" x 5½"
			4	3" x 10½"
	2	17"	4	17" x 17" ⊠
	1	10"	2	10" x 10" ◹

Cutting for Twin Size

Fabric	No. of Strips	Strip Width	No. of Pieces	Piece Size
Background	6	5⅞"	36	5⅞" x 5⅞"
	4	4⅜"	36	4⅜" x 4⅜"
	4	3⅜"	36	3⅜" x 3⅜"
	4	2¼"		
	8	1¾"		
	4	3"	14	3" x 3"
			14	3" x 5½"
Floral	5	5⅞"	28	5⅞" x 5⅞"
	4	4⅜"	28	4⅜" x 4⅜"
	3	3⅜"	28	3⅜" x 3⅜"
	4	2¼"		
Blue	9	1¾"	36 from 3 strips	1¾" x 1¾"
Blue/aqua	5	3"	64	3" x 3"
Yellow	8	1¾"		
	5	3"	22	3" x 3"
			14	3" x 5½"
			4	3" x 10½"
	3	17"	5	17" x 17" ⊠
			2	10" x 10" ◹

Cutting for Queen Size

Fabric	No. of Strips	Strip Width	No. of Pieces	Piece Size
Background	10	5⅞"	55	5⅞" x 5⅞"
	7	4⅜"	55	4⅜" x 4⅜"
	5	3⅜"	55	3⅜" x 3⅜"
	6	2¼"		
	10	1¾"		
	5	3"	18	3" x 3"
			18	3" x 5½"
Floral	8	5⅞"	45	5⅞" x 5⅞"
	5	4⅜"	45	4⅜" x 4⅜"
	5	3⅜"	45	3⅜" x 3⅜"
	6	2¼"		
Blue	11	1¾"	44 from 3 strips	1¾" x 1¾"
Blue/aqua	7	3"	80	3" x 3"
Yellow	10	1¾"		
	6	3"	26	3" x 3"
			18	3" x 5½"
			4	3" x 10½"
	3	17"	6	17" x 17" ⊠
	1	10"	2	10" x 10" ◰

◰ : Cut each square once diagonally.
⊠ : Cut each square twice diagonally.

Block Assembly

1. Sew 2¼"-wide strips of floral and background, right sides together. Press the seam toward the darker fabric. Crosscut the strips at 2¼" intervals.

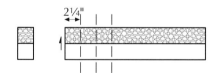

Quilt Size	Strip Units	Segments
Lap	3	36
Twin	4	64
Queen	6	100

2. Sew the units together in pairs as shown to make the four-patch units.

Lap: Make 18.
Twin: Make 32.
Queen: Make 50.

3. Cut each of the 3⅜" background and floral squares once diagonally. Sew background triangles to 2 opposite sides of the four-patch unit. Add floral triangles to the 2 remaining sides. Make sure the four-patch unit is positioned correctly. Reserve the remaining four-patch units for Block 3.

Lap: Make 12.
Twin: Make 24.
Queen: Make 40.

4. Cut each of the 4⅜" background and floral squares once diagonally. Sew the triangles to the pieced unit as shown, making sure the four-patch unit is positioned correctly.

Lap: Make 12.
Twin: Make 24.
Queen: Make 40.

5. Cut each of the 5⅞" background and floral squares once diagonally. Sew the triangles to the pieced unit as shown to complete Block 1.

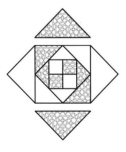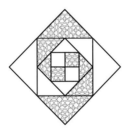

Block 1
Lap: Make 12.
Twin: Make 24.
Queen: Make 40.

6. To make Block 2, fold under ¼" on 2 adjacent sides of a 1¾" blue square; appliqué the square to 1 background corner of a Block 1 as shown.

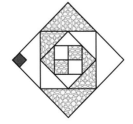

Block 2
Lap: Make 4.
Twin: Make 6.
Queen: Make 8.

7. Add floral and background triangles to the four-patch unit as shown to make the remaining blocks. Always add the floral triangle first; this makes it easier to determine the position of the background triangles.

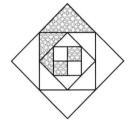

Lap: Make 6.
Twin: Make 8.
Queen: Make 10.

8. Referring to step 6, appliqué a 1¾" blue square to the corner of a block from step 7. Appliqué the square to the corner opposite the floral triangle as shown to complete Block 3.

9. Appliqué a 1¾" blue square to 2 adjacent background corners of a block from step 7 as shown to complete Block 4.

10. Appliqué a 1¾" blue square to 2 adjacent background corners of a block from step 7 as shown to complete Block 5.

Block 3
Lap: Make 2.
Twin: Make 4.
Queen: Make 6.

Block 4
All sizes: Make 2.

Block 5
All sizes: Make 2.

Border and Corner Block Assembly

1. Sew 1¾"-wide strips of background and blue print together. Crosscut at 1¾" intervals.

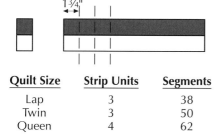

Quilt Size	Strip Units	Segments
Lap	3	38
Twin	3	50
Queen	4	62

2. Sew the units to a 1¾"-wide background strip as shown. Cut them apart, trimming the edges of the long strip even with the pieced unit.

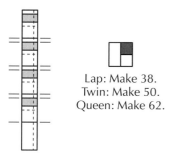

Lap: Make 38.
Twin: Make 50.
Queen: Make 62.

3. Sew 1¾"-wide strips of yellow and blue prints right sides together. Press the seam toward the darker fabric. Crosscut at 1¾" intervals.

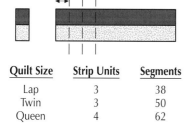

Quilt Size	Strip Units	Segments
Lap	3	38
Twin	3	50
Queen	4	62

4. Sew the units to a 1¾"-wide strip of yellow print as shown. Cut them apart, trimming the edges of the long strip even with the pieced unit.

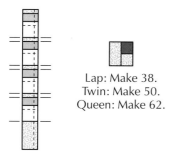

Lap: Make 38.
Twin: Make 50.
Queen: Make 62.

5. Arrange the pieced units with the 3" squares of background, blue/aqua, and yellow, and the 3" x 5½" rectangles of background and yellow as shown. Sew the units together in rows; sew the rows together to make Block 6 for the borders.

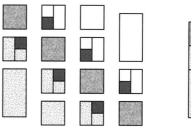

Block 6
Lap: Make 10.
Twin: Make 14.
Queen: Make 18.

6. Arrange the pieced units with the 3" blue/aqua squares, the 3" yellow squares, and the 3" x 10½" yellow rectangles as shown. Sew the units together in rows; sew the rows together to complete Block 7 for the corners.

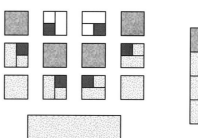

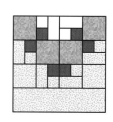

Block 7
All sizes: Make 4.

7. Referring to "Making Pieced Edge Triangles" on page 10, cut a 1¾"-wide strip from one edge of each side setting triangle. Sew a 1¾" blue square to the end of the strip, then reassemble the triangle as shown. Trim the end of the strip even with the base of the triangle.

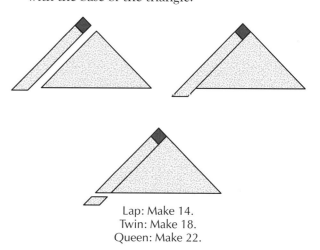

Lap: Make 14.
Twin: Make 18.
Queen: Make 22.

Quilt Top Assembly and Finishing

1. Referring to the photo on page 22 and the quilt plans below, arrange the blocks, side setting triangles, and corner setting triangles as shown.

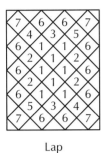

Lap

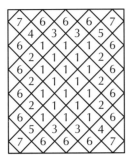

Twin

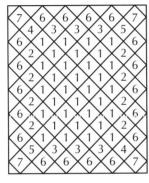

Queen

2. Sew the blocks together in diagonal rows; press the seams in opposite directions from row to row. Sew the rows together.
3. Layer the quilt top with batting and backing; baste.
4. Quilt as desired or follow the quilting suggestion.
5. Bind the edges, then add a label.

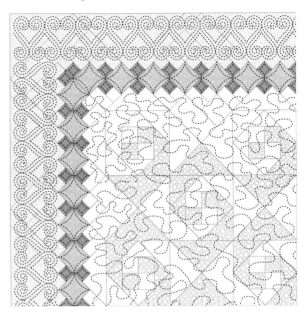

Weather Vane

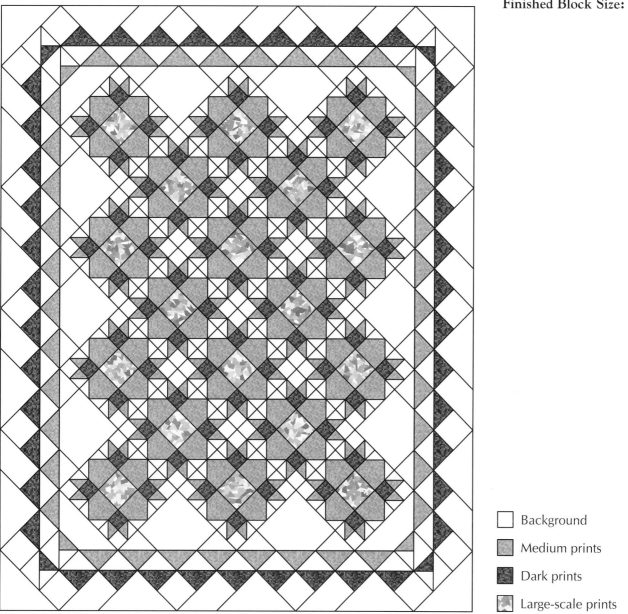

Background

Medium prints

Dark prints

Large-scale prints

Materials: 42"-wide fabric			
FABRIC	**QUILT SIZE**		
	LAP 50" X 62½"	TWIN 62½" x 87½"	QUEEN 87½" X 100"
Background	4 yds.	6¼ yds.	10⅜ yds.
Total assorted medium prints	2 yds.	3½ yds.	6⅝ yds.
Total assorted dark prints	¾ yd.	1⅜ yds.	2⅛ yds.
Total assorted large-scale prints	⅞ yd.	1¾ yds.	3 yds.
Backing	3¼ yds.	5¼ yds.	7⅞ yds.
Batting	58" x 71"	71" x 96"	96" x 108"
Binding	½ yd.	⅝ yd.	¾ yd.

Cutting for Lap Size

Fabric	No. of Strips	Strip Width	No. of Pieces	Piece Size
Background	4	12"	18 right side up	1⅞"-wide bias strips
			11 right side up	3"-wide bias strips
	11	2"	216	2" x 2"
	3	3½"	4	3½" x 9½"
			18	3½" x 3½"
	2	6½"	10	6½" x 6½"
	2	16"	4	16" x 16" ⊠
	1	9"	2	9" x 9" ◩
Medium	3	12"	18 wrong side up	1⅞"-wide bias strips
			4 wrong side up	3"-wide bias strips
	9	3½"	90	3½" x 3½"
Dark	1	12"	7 wrong side up	3"-wide bias strips
	4	2"	72	2" x 2"
Large-scale print	2	3½"	18	3½" x 3½"

Cutting for Twin Size

Fabric	No. of Strips	Strip Width	No. of Pieces	Piece Size
Background	7	12"	39 right side up	1⅞"-wide bias strips
			16 right side up	3"-wide bias strips
	24	2"	468	2" x 2"
	4	3½"	4	3½" x 9½"
			24	3½" x 3½"
	3	6½"	16	6½" x 6½"
	3	16"	5	16" x 16" ⊠
			2	9" x 9" ◩
Medium	5	12"	39 wrong side up	1⅞"-wide bias strips
			6 wrong side up	3"-wide bias strips
	17	3½"	180	3½" x 3½"
Dark	2	12"	10 wrong side up	3"-wide bias strips
	8	2"	156	2" x 2"
Large-scale print	4	3½"	39	3½" x 3½"

◩ : Cut each square once diagonally.
⊠ : Cut each square twice diagonally.

Cutting for Queen Size

Fabric	No. of Strips	Strip Width	No. of Pieces	Piece Size
Background	12	12"	72 right side up	1⅞"-wide bias strips
			21 right side up	3"-wide bias strips
	44	2"	864	2" x 2"
	4	3½"	4	3½" x 9½"
			30	3½" x 3½"
	4	6½"	22	6½" x 6½"
	4	16"	7	16" x 16" ⊠
			2	9" x 9" ◹
Medium	10	12"	72 wrong side up	1⅞"-wide bias strips
			8 wrong side up	3"-wide bias strips
	29	3½"	318	3½" x 3½"
Dark	3	12"	13 wrong side up	3"-wide bias strips
	15	2"	288	2" x 2"
Large-scale print	7	3½"	72	3½" x 3½"

◹: Cut each square once diagonally.
⊠: Cut each square twice diagonally.

Block Assembly

1. Referring to "Making Bias Squares" on page 6, pair 1⅞"-wide bias strips of background and medium prints, right sides together. Sew along both long edges. Cut 2" bias squares from the strips. Press the seams toward the darker fabric. From each medium print/background combination, you will need 16 bias squares—enough for 2 blocks.

Quilt Size	Bias-Strip Units	Bias Squares
Lap	18	144
Twin	39	312
Queen	72	576

2. Referring to "Making Folded Corners" on page 6, sew a 2" background square on 2 adjacent corners of a 3½" medium print square as shown. Make 8 from each print combination (4 units for each block).

Lap: Make 72.
Twin: Make 156.
Queen: Make 288.

3. Arrange 4 folded-corner units, 1 large-scale print 3½" square, 8 bias squares, and 4 dark and 4 background 2" squares as shown. Sew them together to complete Block 1.

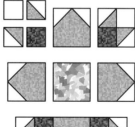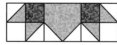

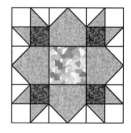

Block 1
Lap: Make 18.
Twin: Make 39.
Queen: Make 72.

Border and Corner Block Assembly

1. Pair 3"-wide bias strips of background and medium prints, right sides together. Sew along both long edges. Cut 3½" bias squares from the strips. Press the seams toward the darker fabric.

Quilt Size	Bias-Strip Units	Bias Squares
Lap	4	20
Twin	6	32
Queen	8	44

2. Repeat step 1 with the 3"-wide bias strips of background and dark prints.

Quilt Size	Bias-Strip Units	Bias Squares
Lap	7	42
Twin	10	60
Queen	13	78

3. Using the folded-corner technique, sew a 3½" medium square on one corner of a 6½" background square.

Lap: Make 10.
Twin: Make 16.
Queen: Make 22.

4. Arrange 1 folded-corner unit, 2 medium bias squares, 2 dark bias squares, and a 3½" background square as shown. Sew them together to make Block 2 for the border.

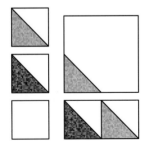
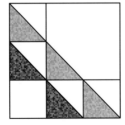

Block 2
Lap: Make 10.
Twin: Make 16.
Queen: Make 22.

5. Using the folded-corner technique, sew a 3½" medium or dark square on both ends of each 3½" x 9½" background rectangle.

All sizes: Make 4.

6. From the leftover background, cut 2 squares, each 4¼" x 4¼", and 4 squares, each 3⅞" x 3⅞". From each of 2 medium prints, cut 1 square, 4¼" x 4¼". From each of 2 dark prints, cut 1 square, 4¼" x 4¼". Referring to "Making Quarter-Square Triangle Units" on page 8, make 8 quarter-square triangle units as shown.

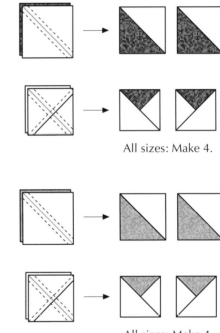

All sizes: Make 4.

All sizes: Make 4.

7. Arrange 1 folded-corner unit, 2 dark 3½" bias squares, 1 medium and 1 dark quarter-square triangle unit, and 2 background 3½" squares as shown. Sew them together to complete Block 3 for the corners.

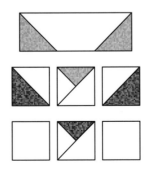
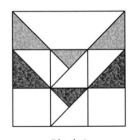

Block 3
All sizes: Make 4.

Quilt Top Assembly and Finishing

1. Referring to "Making Pieced Edge Triangles" on page 10, cut a 3½"-wide strip from the left side of each side setting triangle as shown. Sew a dark bias square to the top edge of the strip, then reassemble the triangle. Trim the strip even with the bottom of the triangle.

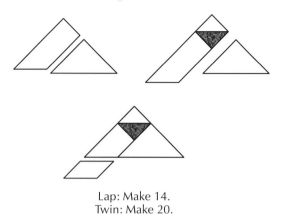

Lap: Make 14.
Twin: Make 20.
Queen: Make 26.

2. Referring to the photo on page 24 and the quilt plans below, arrange the blocks, side setting triangles, and corner setting triangles as shown.

3. Sew the blocks together in diagonal rows; press the seams in opposite directions from row to row. Sew the rows together.

4. Layer the quilt top with batting and backing; baste.
5. Quilt as desired or follow the quilting suggestion.
6. Bind the edges, then add a label.

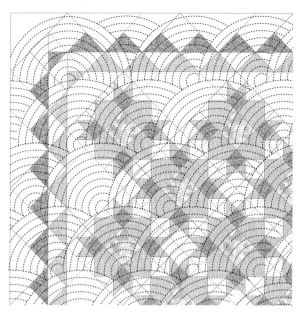

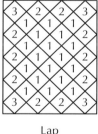

Lap

Twin

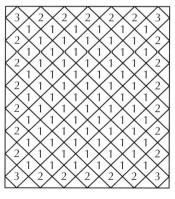

Queen

ADAPTING THE DESIGNS

You are, of course, not limited to using only the block designs shown in this book. You can adapt many of the Painless Borders shown and use them either with other blocks or with different-sized blocks. On the following pages, you will find most of the borders adapted for use with blocks based on a nine-patch, four-patch, or five-patch grid. They look a little different on each size grid; usually the corners change.

The names of the borders describe the shapes and their direction or the name of the quilt; but one border, "Houston Squares," was named for the Houston International Quilt Show where Sally first saw it.

Three of the borders on the quilt patterns—Double Twisted Ribbon, Laurel Wreath, and Quack—do not work on any grid other than the one used in the quilt pattern. But, you can still change the quilt design by using different blocks in the center. As long as the blocks in the center of the quilt are the same size as the blocks in the border, you can choose any blocks for the center, even appliqué blocks.

Changing the designs is easy. "Hovering Hawks" with a "Double Sawtooth Innie Border" on page 18 is based on a four-patch grid. It has four squares across and four squares down. If you want to make an Ohio Star quilt based on a nine-patch grid with the same border, choose the Double Sawtooth Innie Border based on the nine-patch grid and add Ohio Stars in the blank spaces as shown. You can replace some of the Ohio Stars with plain squares if you prefer.

Ohio Star with
Double Sawtooth Innie Border

Blocks Required

Ohio Star and Alternating Plain Squares
with Double Sawtooth Innie Border

Blocks Required

ALL NIGHT LONG BORDER

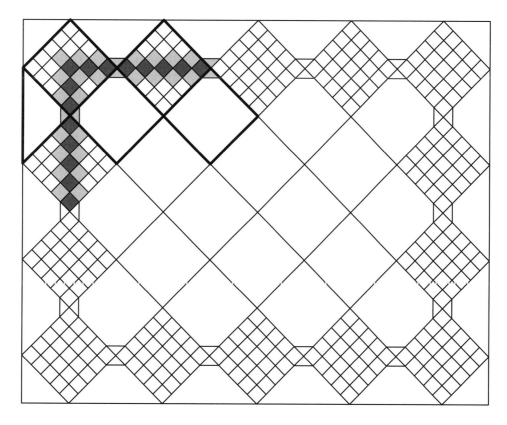

Sawtooth Innie Border

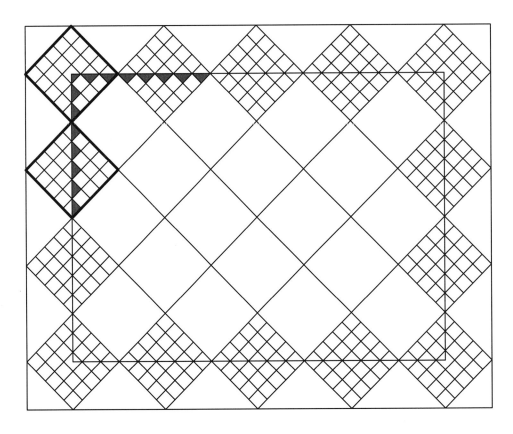

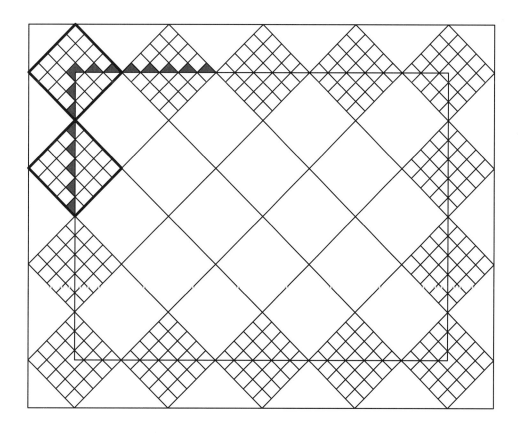

Double Sawtooth Innie Border

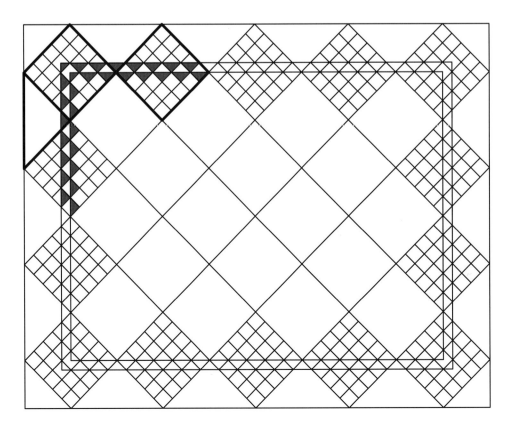

Double Sawtooth Outie Border

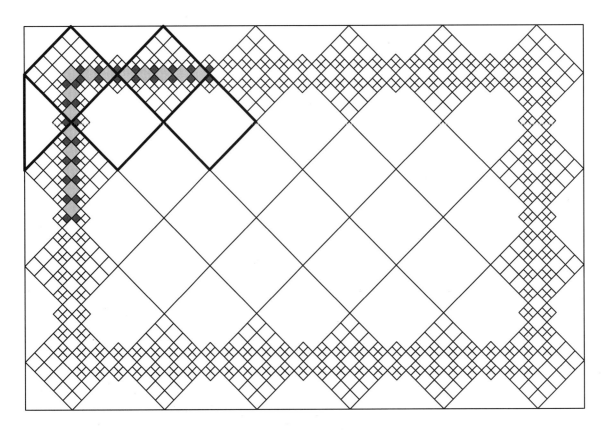

ABOUT THE AUTHORS

BARBARA J. EIKMEIER AND SALLY SCHNEIDER

Barbara J. Eikmeier grew up in a small farming community in northern California. She learned to sew in 4-H at the age of 9 and made her first pieced quilts while in high school in the 1970s. After her marriage in 1984, she took up quilting again and she hasn't looked back!

Relocations with her army-officer husband provide her with opportunities to spread her passion for quilting wherever she lives. Years ago, it was a military assignment in Hawaii that brought Barbara and Sally Schneider together. Barbara recalls taking quilting classes at Sally's kitchen table. In fact, it was Sally who taught her how to use a rotary cutter!

Barbara's quilting interests are broad, but she especially enjoys traditional quilts with an unusual twist. She considers herself a student of quilt history and is a member of the American Quilt Study Group. She is the former owner of The Quilter's Closet, a retail shop, and a member of the American Quilter's Society. She has a particular fondness for teaching quilting to children and is the author of *Kids Can Quilt* (That Patchwork Place, 1997).

Barbara lives at Fort Leavenworth, Kansas, with her husband, Dale, and their two children, Eric and Sarah.

Sally grew up in northeastern Pennsylvania. Her mother taught her to sew when she was a child, and although she has tried many other forms of needlework, quilting has been her passion since 1972.

During twenty years as a military wife, Sally turned to quilting as an outlet for her creativity and a way to meet new people. One of those was Barbara Eikmeier, whom she met while living in Hawaii in the mid-1980s. They became good friends and have continued to quilt together and share ideas. One of Sally's favorite memories is dyeing fabric in her carport with Barbara. They dyed twenty-seven colors, each in six values, and shared the resulting stash of fabric (which Sally keeps neatly stacked on a shelf!)

Sally is the author of *Scrap Happy: Quick-Pieced Scrap Quilts*, *Painless Borders*, and *ScrapMania: More Quick-Pieced Scrap Quilts*, and is a contributor to *Celebrating the Quilt*. She has taught quilting both nationally and internationally. Sally now works as a quilt-book editor for Rodale Press.

Her children are all grown and live in different parts of the country, giving her many options for wonderful vacations. She lives in Breinigsville, Pennsylvania, with her dog, Merlin.

Publications and Products

THAT PATCHWORK PLACE TITLES:

AMERICA'S BEST-LOVED QUILT BOOKS®

All New Copy Art for Quilters
All-Star Sampler • Roxanne Carter
Appliquilt® • Tonee White
Appliquilt® for Christmas • Tonee White
Appliquilt® to Go • Tonee White
Appliquilt® Your ABCs • Tonee White
Around the Block with Judy Hopkins
At Home with Quilts • Nancy J. Martin
Baltimore Bouquets • Mimi Dietrich
Bargello Quilts • Marge Edie
Beyond Charm Quilts
  • Catherine L. McIntee & Tammy L. Porath
Bias Square® Miniatures • Christine Carlson
Blockbender Quilts • Margaret J. Miller
Block by Block • Beth Donaldson
Borders by Design • Paulette Peters
The Border Workbook • Janet Kime
Calicoes & Quilts Unlimited
  • Judy Betts Morrison
The Cat's Meow • Janet Kime
Celebrate! with Little Quilts • Alice Berg,
  Mary Ellen Von Holt & Sylvia Johnson
Celebrating the Quilt
Class-Act Quilts
*Classic Quilts with Precise Foundation
  Piecing* • Tricia Lund & Judy Pollard
Color: The Quilter's Guide • Christine Barnes
Colourwash Quilts • Deirdre Amsden
Crazy but Pieceable • Hollie A. Milne
Crazy Rags • Deborah Brunner
Decorate with Quilts & Collections
  • Nancy J. Martin
Down the Rotary Road with Judy Hopkins
Dress Daze • Judy Murrah
Dressed by the Best
The Easy Art of Appliqué
  • Mimi Dietrich & Roxi Eppler
Easy Machine Paper Piecing • Carol Doak
*Easy Mix & Match Machine Paper
  Piecing* • Carol Doak
Easy Paper-Pieced Keepsake Quilts
  • Carol Doak
Easy Reversible Vests • Carol Doak
Easy Seasonal Wall Quilts • Deborah J.
  Moffett-Hall
A Fine Finish • Cody Mazuran
*Five- and Seven-Patch Blocks & Quilts for
  the ScrapSaver* • Judy Hopkins
*Four-Patch Blocks & Quilts for the
  ScrapSaver* • Judy Hopkins
Freedom in Design • Mia Rozmyn
From a Quilter's Garden • Gabrielle Swain
Go Wild with Quilts • Margaret Rolfe
Go Wild with Quilts—Again! • Margaret Rolfe
Great Expectations • Karey Bresenhan
  with Alice Kish & Gay E. McFarland
Hand-Dyed Fabric Made Easy
  • Adriene Buffington
Happy Endings • Mimi Dietrich
Honoring the Seasons • Takako Onoyama
Jacket Jazz • Judy Murrah

Jacket Jazz Encore • Judy Murrah
The Joy of Quilting
  • Joan Hanson & Mary Hickey
Kids Can Quilt • Barbara J. Eikmeier
Life in the Country with Country Threads
  • Mary Tendall & Connie Tesene
Little Quilts • Alice Berg, Mary Ellen Von Holt &
  Sylvia Johnson
Lively Little Logs • Donna McConnell
Living with Little Quilts • Alice Berg,
  Mary Ellen Von Holt & Sylvia Johnson
The Log Cabin Design Workbook
  • Christal Carter
Lora & Company • Lora Rocke
Loving Stitches • Jeana Kimball
*Machine Needlelace and Other
  Embellishment Techniques* • Judy Simmons
Machine Quilting Made Easy • Maurine Noble
*Magic Base Blocks for Unlimited Quilt
  Designs* • Patty Barney & Cooky Schock
Miniature Baltimore Album Quilts
  • Jenifer Buechel
Mirror Manipulations • Gail Valentine
More Jazz from Judy Murrah
More Quilts for Baby • Ursula Reikes
More Strip-Pieced Watercolor Magic
  • Deanna Spingola
*Nine-Patch Blocks & Quilts for the
  ScrapSaver* • Judy Hopkins
No Big Deal • Deborah L. White
Once upon a Quilt
  • Bonnie Kaster & Virginia Athey
Patchwork Pantry
  • Suzette Halferty & Carol C. Porter
A Perfect Match • Donna Lynn Thomas
A Pioneer Doll and Her Quilts • Mary Hickey
Press for Success • Myrna Giesbrecht
Quilted for Christmas, Book II
Quilted for Christmas, Book III
Quilted for Christmas, Book IV
Quilted Landscapes • Joan Blalock
Quilted Legends of the West
  • Judy Zehner & Kim Mosher
Quilted Sea Tapestries • Ginny Eckley
A Quilter's Ark • Margaret Rolfe
Quilting Design Sourcebook • Dorothy Osler
Quilting Makes the Quilt • Lee Cleland
Quilting Up a Storm • Lydia Quigley
Quilts: An American Legacy • Mimi Dietrich
Quilts for Baby • Ursula Reikes
Quilts for Red-Letter Days • Janet Kime
Quilts from Nature • Joan Colvin
Quilts Say It Best • Eileen Westfall
Refrigerator Art Quilts • Jennifer Paulson
Rotary Riot • Judy Hopkins & Nancy J. Martin
Rotary Roundup
  • Judy Hopkins & Nancy J. Martin
Round Robin Quilts
  • Pat Magaret & Donna Slusser
Sensational Settings • Joan Hanson
Sew a Work of Art Inside and Out
  • Charlotte Bird
*Shortcuts: A Concise Guide to Rotary
  Cutting* • Donna Lynn Thomas
Show Me How to Paper-Piece • Carol Doak
Simply Scrappy Quilts • Nancy J. Martin

Small Talk • Donna Lynn Thomas
Square Dance • Martha Thompson
Start with Squares • Martha Thompson
Strip-Pieced Watercolor Magic
  • Deanna Spingola
Stripples • Donna Lynn Thomas
Stripples Strikes Again! • Donna Lynn Thomas
Strips That Sizzle • Margaret J. Miller
Sunbonnet Sue All Through the Year
  • Sue Linker
Template-Free® Quilts and Borders
  • Trudie Hughes
Threadplay with Libby Lehman • Libby Lehman
Through the Window & Beyond
  • Lynne Edwards
The Total Bedroom • Donna Babylon
Traditional Blocks Meet Appliqué
  • Deborah J. Moffett-Hall
Traditional Quilts with Painless Borders
  • Sally Schneider & Barbara J. Eikmeier
Transitions • Andrea Balosky
Tropical Punch • Marilyn Dorwart
True Style • Peggy True
Variations in Chenille • Nannette Holmberg
Victorian Elegance • Lezette Thomason
Watercolor Impressions
  • Pat Magaret & Donna Slusser
Watercolor Quilts
  • Pat Magaret & Donna Slusser
Weave It! Quilt It! Wear It!
  • Mary Anne Caplinger
Welcome to the North Pole
  • Piece O' Cake Designs
Whimsies & Whynots • Mary Lou Weidman
WOW! Wool-on-Wool Folk Art Quilts
  • Janet Carija Brandt
Your First Quilt Book (or it should be!)
  • Carol Doak

4", 6", 8" & metric Bias Square® • BiRangle™
Ruby Beholder® • ScrapMaster • Bias Stripper™
Shortcuts to America's Best-Loved Quilts (video)

FIBER STUDIO PRESS TITLES:

Complex Cloth • Jane Dunnewold
Dyes & Paints • Elin Noble
*Erika Carter: Personal Imagery
  in Art Quilts* • Erika Carter
*Fine Art Quilts: Work by Artists
  of the Contemporary QuiltArt
  Association*
Inspiration Odyssey • Diana Swim Wessel
The Nature of Design • Joan Colvin
Thread Magic • Ellen Anne Eddy
*Velda Newman: A Painter's Approach
  to Quilt Design* • Velda Newman with
  Christine Barnes